The Rookies Guide to PSI Talent

Matthew Sprange

Contents

Credits

Editor
Alexander Fennell

Cover Art
Greg Staples

Interior Illustrations
Bret Ewins (3, 5, 7, 8, 10, 12, 13, 15, 16, 18, 21, 34, 37, 39, 43, 45, 49, 51, 53, 55, 59, 63, 67, 71, 83, 87, 88, 90-92), John Caliber (69, 72, 73, 75-82, 84, 85,), Ron Smith (4, 24, 26, 27, 29, 30, 64)

Graphic Design
Anne Stokes

Proof Reading
Ian Barstow

Judge Dredd created by John Wagner and Carlos Ezquerra

Introduction

Only a tiny fraction of the population within Mega-City One have any psi-talent at all. Through the power of their mind alone, these rare individuals are able to influence the thoughts of another, levitate inanimate objects or gaze into the future to witness their own fate and that of others. Ever since the Atomic War of 2070, the incidence of psi-talent within the population of virtually every city in the world has steadily been increasing – as have the danger associated with this unpredictable skill.

The Justice Department of Mega-City One keeps an iron grip on the rise of citizens who possess psi-talent, or psykers, as they are known. Though psi-judges are a welcome and necessary addition to the forces of justice, the misuse of psi-talent has been responsible for some of the greatest tragedies ever to have befallen the city. The Judge Child Expedition, the Zombie War and Necropolis all have direct links with rogue psykers and psychic entities. Psi-Division therefore has many operatives who constantly scan the thought patterns of the entire population of the city, searching for those citizens who pose the greatest potential danger. These individuals often join the ranks of the psi-judges if they are found at an early enough age, but many are sentenced to life in the psi-cubes – a harsh and drastic measure that destroys their freedom but ultimately protects every other citizen in the city.

Rogue psykers still exist though, and there are all too many who are ready to grant them protection in exchange for their unique talents. Criminal organisations will work hard to protect any psyker under their influence, from both the Justice Department and rival gangs. Mutants displaying psi-talent are regularly smuggled into Mega-City One, though they rarely escape the judges for long, particularly if they also display physical abnormalities. Some of the other city states in the world have much freer policy with regards to psykers and so the Justice Department's Immigration Division must constantly be wary of visitors who may possess psi-talent entering Mega-City One.

The growing incidence of psi-talent within Mega-City One and the surrounding environs of the Cursed Earth may yet prove to be the greatest danger the city has yet to face, with past disasters but a prelude to utter catastrophe.

For every judge working to suppress the effect of psi-talent amongst the citizens, there may be ten perps all too ready to take advantage of the supernatural in order to make a few credits. What price will be paid for meddling in the unknown is yet to be determined.

The Rookie's Guide to Psi-Talent

This rules supplement is a comprehensive guide to psi-talent and its users in the Judge Dredd roleplaying game. Whether they play judges or citizens, any player with a psi-talented character will find new ways to increase the capabilities of his powers. Newly-created psi-talented characters may now opt to become specialists, focussing on one specific area of psi-talent, while others may enjoy the benefits of a greatly increased selection of psi-powers and new equipment designed to boost their talent beyond all human endurance. Psi-judges may specialise further by joining the Exorcist Squads of Psi-Division and there are many new prestige classes for citizens who possess psi-talent. Games Masters will find they have a wide variety of new tools to use when detailing any new scenario. Psi-talented perps can challenge judges or citizens alike in entirely new ways and the psychic entities in Chapter 7 will provide many a great nemesis for characters of all levels.

The rules within *The Rookie's Guide to Psi-Talent* do not replace the rules in the *Judge Dredd Rulebook* but, rather, build upon them to greatly expand any character who possesses psi-talent in the game. Players will soon learn that a potent psi-talent leaves few physical marks and that even the lowliest juve can become a terrible enemy if provoked.

The Psi-Flux

Simply put in layman's terms, the psi-flux is the range of psionic frequencies used by psykers as they manifest their remarkable psychic powers. Throughout the world and across the expanse of time, the psi-flux has been called many things by those capable of psi-talent – the Source, the Wellspring of Creation and the Force, to name but a few. It is the raw energy fundamental to this universe and others that a tiny fraction of humanity is able to access and manipulate to affect the world around themselves. Whenever a psyker uses his talent, he is accessing energies invisible to normal humans.

It is often believed that psi-talent comes purely from within the mind of a psyker, though this is not quite true. Psi-talented citizens have extraordinarily developed brains that are capable of both picking up and manipulating the psionic frequencies of the flux. In a way, all humans have this potential – most citizens, at some point in their lives, have a 'sense' that something is wrong or experience incredible bouts of luck. During these times, they are probably, and unwittingly, picking up on strong frequencies within the psi-flux. However, without the psychic gene that develops the brain of a true psyker, they will never be able to access it at will or manipulate it to their own ends. That is the mark of a genuine psychic, one who can not only consistently pick up the frequencies of the psi-flux, but also draw them into his mind, bend or shape the energies to his will, and then release them to affect the real world. A strong-willed psyker has the capability to invade minds, dominate personalities, set spontaneous fires, open portals to other dimensions and hurl solid objects through the air with nothing more than a simple thought.

Psi-talented citizens are no strangers to Mega-City One and their numbers have been steadily increasing since the Atom War of 2070, alongside the incidence of physical mutations within the population. The Justice Department, however, does not consider the presence of psi-talent alone reason to deem a citizen a mutant – indeed, while the vast majority of mutations are random, if not downright dangerous, psi-talent seems, in comparison, to be remarkably stable. Though such citizens are placed under stresses that no mundane human could ever hope to understand, they are not, as a breed, psychotic or unstable. There are, of course, exceptions to this rule.

A citizen found to possess psi-talent will not be immediately exiled into the Cursed Earth, as would be the case for any other mutation. Instead, they are tracked and hunted down by operatives from the Justice Department's Psi-Division, for while rogue psykers are capable of a great many crimes that might otherwise remain undetectable, when properly monitored they have an intrinsic use to Mega-City One as a whole. Captured young enough, particularly strong-willed juves may find themselves eligible to join the ranks of psi-judges, though few survive the training process and fewer actually graduate. These psi-judges form the frontline of psychic defence for the entire city, using their unique talents to aid in criminal investigations, hunt down rogue psykers or peer into the future to watch for threats to Mega-City One. Those who do not make the grade as psi-judges, for reasons of old age, uncontrollable talent or simple mental instability are doomed to be forever incarcerated in the psi-cubes, secure facilities that keep them far from the normal population and thus unable to exercise their powers.

DIRTY SMART-ASS PSI! I'M GOING TO RIP THAT PRETTY FACE OFF!

Criminal Psykers

Given the Justice Department's no-tolerance stance on rogue psykers and the fate most receive at their hands, it is unsurprising that many choose to hide from Psi-Division. There are many street gangs and criminal organisations that, despite any prejudice towards psi-talent, are more than happy to welcome a rogue into their ranks. In return for protection and security from the judges, the rogue psykers can provide perps with an incredible range of abilities that would otherwise not be possible – a beleaguered and outnumbered street gang may suddenly turn upon its rivals and begin hammering them in a series of rumbles when supported by a psyker who can distract and even kill the enemy with but a single thought. Larger organisations can always find use for a good telepath in business negotiations, granting them a huge advantage when making multi-million credit deals. Psykers who can see into the future, for however short a time, may be regularly sought after by any number of citizens.

Given their range of supernatural abilities, it is perhaps somewhat surprising that psi-talented perps do not rise very far in any street gang or organisation – it is incredibly rare to find a criminal mastermind who is also a psyker, even if he has many such citizens in his employ. However, the rogue psyker risks far, far more than his criminal counterpart. Any group of perps caught and arrested by the judges for a crime such as assault, can expect to be placed in an iso-cube for a number of years. At some point though, they can expect to be released. If a rogue psyker is among them, however, and his talent is detected by the judges, he will be sent to the psi-cubes and never be released, no matter what his true crime was. Rogue psykers tend, therefore, to stay within the shadows of street gangs and criminal organisations, rarely straying into any area or activity that puts them at risk of discovery.

This is not, by any means, an easy life. The operatives of Psi-Division constantly monitor the psi-flux for any irregularities and eddies that would indicate the use of psi-talent in their area. Psi-crime is on the increase in Mega-City One and the Justice Department is well aware that even its highly trained street judges may not be capable of dealing with a powerful psi-talented citizen. Psi-Division is also ever-alert for rogue psykers attempting to push their powers a little too far, for this can have catastrophic consequences for the rest of the population of Mega-City One. The misuse of the psi-flux can open doorways to other worlds and dimensions, where creatures of unbelievable evil and power dwell. Mega-City One has endured the incursions of mighty psychic entities from other dimensions several times in the past, and every event results in massive destruction and death on a huge scale. Psi-Division does not simply track down rogue psykers for the crimes they may be tempted to commit – each psi-talented citizen who remains out of their control represents a potential but very real threat to the city as a whole.

Specialists

The vast majority of psi-talented citizens are considered to be unspecialised – they have a good grasp of what the psi-flux means and how to manipulate it, but their powers are broad and typically unfocussed. This in no way makes them any less of a psyker and some of the greatest telepaths to have emerged in Mega-City One's history have been unspecialised. Most discover their powers by accident and choose not to probe too deeply into the nature of the psi-flux, preferring instead to concentrate on the actual application of their new found abilities.

Other psi-talented citizens, whether through training, mental discipline or simply being freaks of nature, are regarded as specialists among psykers. They focus their minds on to one single aspect of the psi-flux and strive to understand everything they can about their talent. Such psykers are greatly limited in the range of powers they may employ when compared to their unspecialised counterparts, but they tend to be far stronger within their own field.

To date, Psi-Division officially recognises five specialised forms of psi-talent – dimensionalism, pre-cog, pyrokinesis, telekinesis and telepathy. Outside of the Justice Department, there is some dispute as to the veracity of such classifications in the face of something as huge and mind-boggling as the psi-flux. Some consider empaths or the dream-invading hypnopaths to be separate specialisations, rather than being inherently connected to telepathy as Psi-Division doctrine would have it. Furthermore, there are always rumours and stories of rogue psykers demonstrating never before seen powers that can only be part of another, yet unknown, specialisation. This is where the tales of temporalists and psykers who can directly access computer systems come from.

Dimensions

It has been long known that the psi-flux and the presence of other dimensions are heavily connected, though the nature of this link has never been fully understood. Some theorise that the actual, physical material of the psi-flux, such as it is, forms one huge dimension that contains all possible universes. Others believe that the psi-flux is the stuff of creation that lies between the different dimensions and connects one to all. The entire truth may never be known, no matter how far psi-science progresses.

There are several known dimensions to be found in the records of the Justice Department, though none are made common knowledge to the citizens of the city, and there are few psi-judges who do not suspect there are actually millions more waiting to be discovered.

Perhaps the most famous of these dimensions is Deadworld, the home of the Dark Judges, Death, Fear, Fire and Mortis. Now lifeless after the Dark Judges' purge, it is a place of inherent evil and classified as being off-limits to any dimensionalist psi-judge. Others have included alternative Mega-City Ones and places that can only be described as demon worlds, hellish places that harbour all manner of evil and twisted life forms. The standard laws of physics need not apply on any other dimension beyond the real world and any psyker actually choosing to travel between them should possess an inflexible will and an utter grip on sanity, for both will be sorely tested.

Actual travel between dimensions is rare, however, and the Justice Department is reluctant to grant any judge permission to do so except in the most extreme and city-threatening of emergencies. There is simply too much that can go wrong. Powerful psykers can, however, manipulate the barriers between the real world and other dimensions in order to gain access to the psi-flux directly. In doing so, they toy with dark arts that perhaps mankind was never meant to even know about, much less use to satisfy his own whims. Creatures, known as psychic entities, dwell within other dimensions and most look upon the real world with hungry eyes. Most are small and relatively fragile but even the least of these can rend a citizen apart within seconds. The most powerful are immortal beings of awesome power, such as the Dark Judges. When a psi-talented citizen begins toying with the barriers between dimensions, he risks opening a portal that psychic entities can slip through, and so unleash a literal hell upon Mega-City One. It is this threat, more than mundane criminal activities, that makes Psi-Division work so hard to trap every rogue psyker they can find. The risks are too great to do otherwise.

Psychic Entities

While the actual nature of the dimensions is open to much speculation and debate, Psi-Division has quite an extensive catalogue of the various psychic entities that dwell within other worlds and have broken through to the real world. Ghosts and poltergeists are relatively common and fairly well understood by psi-judges but there are far darker entities waiting for a chance to break

through to the real world and wreck havoc upon mankind. Demons, avatars and even gods do indeed exist and represent perhaps the greatest threat to humans outside of their own capacity to destroy themselves. Incursions are, thankfully, rare and full-blown assaults from other dimensions virtually unheard of. However, psychic entities possess powers outside of normal human experience and even highly trained street judges may be swept aside by an immortal creature.

Another rare occurrence, but one slowly growing in numbers of reported cases, is that of demonic possession. It has been known for many years that some 'demons' or psychic entities from other dimensions have the capability to actually possess a human being for extended periods of time. In doing so, they can utterly destroy their victim but in return gain a steady foothold within the real world from which they can plot, plan and enact their vision of destruction upon mankind. While not usually as powerful as manifesting themselves bodily in the real world, cases of demonic possession can prove to be extremely dangerous as investigating judges may mistake the creature for an unusual psi-talented citizen, not realising their error until it is far too late.

Psi-Division has many specialists within its ranks, but the battle against psychic entities and cases of possession falls squarely to the exorcist judges. Highly respected even by other powerful psi-operatives, the exorcist judges represent the first and last line of defence in Mega-City One against psychic entities. Armed with the very best equipment available to Psi-Division and heavily trained in the nature of the supernatural creatures they must regularly battle against, every member of the Exorcist Squad is conditioned to lay down his life for the city if that is what is required to end the menace. Even so, there are never any shortage of volunteers for the high profile Exorcist Squad, though even psi-judges often lack the mental endurance and will to succeed in the vigorous training that prepares the exorcist judges for the titanic battle of wills they must engage in every time they investigate another case of possession or appearance of a psychic entity in the real world.

Specialists

Of the few citizens who actually possess psi-talent, only a tiny fraction have either access to, or the ability to take advantage of, specialist training. Most are condemned to use only a few specific powers that come naturally to them, usually simple telepathic or pre-cog abilities that many psykers are able to manipulate with relative ease.

Specialists, however, concentrate their psychic talent into just one field of ability, either dimensionalist, pre-cog, pyrokine, telekine or telepath domains. By virtue of training or pure natural ability, they are able to mass great reserves of power that dwarfs those psykers who merely dabble in psi-talent. The drawback is that specialists have little ability beyond their chosen field of psi-talent. A dabbler of the psychic can, potentially, stumble across any power accessible to specialists. The specialists themselves are greatly restricted in the powers they can learn but will be far more potent within their field.

A great many new psi-powers are introduced into the game of Judge Dredd in the next chapter. Unlike those in the *Judge Dredd Rulebook*, however, the new powers have been divided into six categories – general, dimensionalist, pre-cog, pyrokine, telekine and telepath. Those in the general category are a mixture of simple powers that any character with psi-talent may learn to control. Powers in the other categories are specialist powers that many characters will be restricted from taking.

All psi-powers in the *Judge Dredd Rulebook* are from this point considered to be general powers, mainly a mixture of simple telepath and pre-cog abilities that most psykers have the potential to obtain.

Unspecialised Psykers

Characters with psi-talent who do not choose to become specialists during character creation follow all the normal

CONSIDERING A CRIMINAL ACT?

DON'T EVEN THINK ABOUT IT!

PSI-DIVISION
"IT'S THE THOUGHT THAT COUNTS"

McCARTHY

psi-talent rules detailed in Chapter 7 of the *Judge Dredd Rulebook*. They may freely choose powers from any of the general or specialist categories. This allows such characters to have a broad range of powers at their disposal though they will have fewer in total in comparison to a specialist.

Becoming a Specialist

Any character with psi-talent may choose to become a specialist during character creation – they may not choose to become a specialist at any time later in life. Each type of specialist (dimensionalist, pre-cog, pyrokine, telekine or telepath) has a basic prerequisite that the character must possess in order to qualify to become a specialist in that field. In order to become a telekine, for example, a character must have a Dexterity score of 15 or greater.

A specialist may only ever select powers from the general or his specialised categories, greatly limiting the range of powers available to him. The telekine discussed above would only be able choose powers from the general and telekine categories, for instance.

In return, specialists gain two bonuses that allow them a greater capability in their chosen field than can ever be attained by an unspecialised psyker. When-ever using a power from their specialised field, they gain a +2 bonus to the DC of any saving throw a subject must make to resist it. In effect, the saving throw against any specialised power used by a specialist is equal to the level of the power + his Charisma modifier + 12. General powers used by specialists do not gain this bonus.

Specialists also receive extra powers, as shown on the table below. These bonus powers must be from the character's specialised category and may not be general

powers. The powers gained normally as the character advances in level may be specialised or general as the character sees fit. This not only gives the specialist a greater number of powers to choose from in total, but also gives him access to higher level powers sooner than an unspecialised counterpart.

For example Psi-Judge Gibbs is weighing up his options as he enters Psi-School. If he remains unspecialised, then by the time he graduates (3rd level), he will know 2 0-level powers and 2 1st level powers. However, if he chooses to become a specialist, then upon reaching 3rd level, he will know 3 0-level powers and 3 1st level powers. In addition, when he reaches 4th level, he will gain not only another 0-level power, as an unspecialised Psi-Judge would, but also a 2nd level power. He will be greatly limited in the choice of powers he may select though.

Dimensionalists

Prerequisite: Intelligence 15+

The dimensionalist is a strange psyker, one who is able to peer into the psi-flux itself and manipulate the energies present in other worlds and other dimensions beyond normal human experience. This is an extremely dangerous field for a psyker to pursue for they are literally dabbling in arts man was not meant to know. Strange beings lurk beyond the veils of reality, waiting for an inexperienced dimensionalist to weaken the boundaries of this world just enough for them to break through and cause havoc. Dimensionalists may take the form of demonologists seeking to access greater power through the manipulation and control of awesome psychic entities, exorcists desperately trying to stop the plans of those dimensionalists who look to bring catastrophe down on Mankind, or even just dabblers who draw energy directly from the psi-flux for their own ends without having any idea of the horrors they may bring upon themselves and others.

Specialist Psi-Judge Power Table

Level	Power Pts/Day	0	1	2	3	4	5	6	7	8	9
1	2	2 + s	s	-	-	-	-	-	-	-	-
2	3	2 + s	1 + s	-	-	-	-	-	-	-	-
3	4	2 + s	2 + s	-	-	-	-	-	-	-	-
4	7	3 + s	2 + s	s	-	-	-	-	-	-	-
5	10	3 + s	2 + s	1 + s	-	-	-	-	-	-	-
6	15	4 + s	2 + s	1 + s	s	-	-	-	-	-	-
7	20	4 + s	3 + s	2 + s	1 + s	-	-	-	-	-	-
8	27	5 + s	3 + s	2 + s	1 + s	s	-	-	-	-	-
9	34	5 + s	3 + s	2 + s	2 + s	1 + s	-	-	-	-	-
10	43	6 + s	3 + s	2 + s	2 + s	1 + s	s	-	-	-	-
11	52	6 + s	3 + s	3 + s	2 + s	2 + s	1 + s	-	-	-	-
12	63	7 + s	3 + s	3 + s	2 + s	2 + s	1 + s	s	-	-	-
13	74	7 + s	4 + s	3 + s	3 + s	2 + s	2 + s	1 + s	-	-	-
14	87	7 + s	4 + s	3 + s	3 + s	2 + s	2 + s	1 + s	s	-	-
15	100	7 + s	4 + s	3 + s	3 + s	3 + s	2 + s	2 + s	1 + s	-	-
16	115	7 + s	4 + s	4 + s	3 + s	3 + s	2 + s	2 + s	1 + s	s	-
17	130	7 + s	4 + s	4 + s	3 + s	3 + s	3 + s	2 + s	2 + s	1 + s	-
18	147	7 + s	4 + s	4 + s	4 + s	3 + s	3 + s	2 + s	2 + s	1 + s	s
19	164	7 + s	4 + s	4 + s	4 + s	3 + s	3 + s	3 + s	2 + s	2 + s	1 + s
20	183	7 + s	4 + s	4 + s	4 + s	4 + s	3 + s	3 + s	2 + s	2 + s	1 + s

Specialist Rogue Psyker Power Table

Level	PowerPts/Day	0	1	2	3	4	5	6	7	8	9
1	2	1 + s	s	-	-	-	-	-	-	-	-
2	3	2 + s	1 + s	-	-	-	-	-	-	-	-
3	4	2 + s	1 + s	-	-	-	-	-	-	-	-
4	7	2 + s	1 + s	s	-	-	-	-	-	-	-
5	10	3 + s	2 + s	1 + s	-	-	-	-	-	-	-
6	15	3 + s	2 + s	1 + s	s	-	-	-	-	-	-
7	20	3 + s	2 + s	1 + s	1 + s	-	-	-	-	-	-
8	27	4 + s	2 + s	2 + s	1 + s	s	-	-	-	-	-
9	34	4 + s	2 + s	2 + s	1 + s	1 + s	-	-	-	-	-
10	43	4 + s	3 + s	2 + s	2 + s	1 + s	s	-	-	-	-
11	52	5 + s	3 + s	2 + s	2 + s	1 + s	1 + s	-	-	-	-
12	63	5 + s	3 + s	2 + s	2 + s	2 + s	1 + s	s	-	-	-
13	74	5 + s	3 + s	3 + s	2 + s	2 + s	1 + s	1 + s	-	-	-
14	87	6 + s	3 + s	3 + s	2 + s	2 + s	2 + s	1 + s	s	-	-
15	100	6 + s	3 + s	3 + s	3 + s	2 + s	2 + s	1 + s	1 + s	-	-
16	115	6 + s	3 + s	3 + s	3 + s	2 + s	2 + s	2 + s	1 + s	s	-
17	130	7 + s	3 + s	3 + s	3 + s	3 + s	2 + s	2 + s	1 + s	1 + s	-
18	147	7 + s	4 + s	3 + s	3 + s	3 + s	2 + s	2 + s	2 + s	1 + s	-
19	164	7 + s	4 + s	3 + s	3 + s	3 + s	3 + s	2 + s	2 + s	1 + s	s
20	183	7 + s	4 + s	3 + s	3 + s	3 + s	3 + s	2 + s	2 + s	2 + s	1 + s

s = Bonus specialist power.

Pre-Cogs

Prerequisite: Wisdom 15+

After telepaths, pre-cogs are amongst the most common types of specialists in psi-talent and, indeed, the Justice Department's Psi-Division works hard to constantly train new operatives as others retire or succumb to their visions. A pre-cog has the ability to literally see into both the past and the future, an obvious benefit during criminal investigations. Few pre-cogs attain the ability to conjure lucid visions at will, however, and the practice has always been viewed more as an art than a science. The dreams of powerful pre-cogs are closely monitored and they are required to report everything they see. Outside of the Justice Department, there are many weak pre-cogs who receive nothing more than a 'bad feeling' when considering a course of action or when talking to a citizen destined to meet his fate in the near future. In the Cursed Earth, pre-cogs often enjoy some status as fortune tellers in the many scattered settlements throughout the wilderness where the Laws of Mega-City One do not require they submit to Psi-Division.

Pyrokines

Prerequisite: Constitution 15+

The pyrokine is closely related to the telekine in his mental ability, but instead of concentrating on mind over matter, he focuses on mind over energy. By agitating particles in any solid object, the pyrokine can cause fire to spring up spontaneously, with tremendous force if he possesses a strong will. There are few pyrokines within the Justice Department as the discipline has few applications in Law enforcement, but there exist a few rogue psykers with an affinity to fire who pose a tremendous threat to Mega-City One. A perp able to burn a judge just by looking at him is a dangerous citizen to apprehend unless an equally powerful psi-judge is also present to negate his powers.

Telekines

Prerequisite: Dexterity 15+

Telekines are one of the rarest forms of specialists, as their field is one of immense will and dedication – a telekine has the ability of mind over matter, being able to move solid objects with thought alone. Skilled telekines concentrate on moving not only larger and heavier objects as they progress in their training, but also smaller and finer things. The greatest telekines are capable of both throwing aside huge vehicles or manipulating tiny air particles in order to form a defensive shield or repel attack. It is often said that most telekines are, in fact, clinically insane though this is something of a misconception. There are not many insane telepaths who have the precision or strength of personality to be able to master telekinetic powers and so most simply continue as unspecialised psykers who have managed to learn a few telekinetic powers.

Telepaths

Prerequisite: Charisma 15+

Of all the specialists, telepaths are by far the most common. The discipline seems to be the easiest to achieve as its study is a natural progression from the talent all psykers are capable of manifesting, regardless of their upbringing or teaching. The strength of the telepath is the ability to read, influence, control and dominate the mind of another. A skilled telepath is capable of controlling entire mobs of citizens with a simple thought, delving into the mind of a victim to uncover their deepest secrets or even altering the memories of another. The most famous telepath of all, Psi-Judge Anderson, is noted as being one of the most powerful operatives of Psi-Div and is testimony that specialists can harbour tremendous powers, given sufficient skill and training.

Bonus Power Points

Some of the psychic entities detailed in Chapter 7 of this supplement have psi-talent that greatly outweighs that normally achievable by even highly-trained humans. The bonus power points table on page 13 of the *Judge Dredd Rulebook* has therefore been extended to take into account enormous Charisma scores.

Bonus Power Points Table

Charisma Score	Bonus Power Points (by Character Level or Hit Dice)									
	1-2	3-4	5-6	7-8	9-10	11-12	13-14	15-16	17-18	19-20
10-11	-	-	-	-	-	-	-	-	-	-
12-13	1	-	-	-	-	-	-	-	-	-
14-15	1	3	-	-	-	-	-	-	-	-
16-17	1	3	5	-	-	-	-	-	-	-
18-19	1	3	5	7	-	-	-	-	-	-
20-21	3	3	5	7	9	-	-	-	-	-
22-23	3	5	5	7	9	11	-	-	-	-
24-25	3	5	7	7	9	11	13	-	-	-
26-27	3	5	7	9	9	11	13	15	-	-
28-29	5	5	7	9	11	11	13	15	17	-
30-31	5	7	7	9	11	13	13	15	17	19
32-33	5	7	9	9	11	13	15	15	17	19
34-35	5	7	9	11	11	13	15	17	17	19
36-37	7	7	9	11	13	13	15	17	19	19
38-39	7	9	9	11	13	15	15	17	19	21
40-41	7	9	11	11	13	15	17	17	19	21

Etc. . .

Psi-Powers

This chapter adds a great many new powers available to any character with psi-talent, greatly widening the scope of their abilities. No longer restricted to the powers listed in the *Judge Dredd Rulebook*, a psi-talented character can now accomplish a staggering array of possibilities with the force of his mind alone.

All the new powers in this chapter are divided into one of six categories. Any psi-talented character may access powers from the General category, which also includes those powers detailed in the *Judge Dredd Rulebook*. Only unspecialised characters may access the powers in all the Dimensionalist, Pre-cog, Pyrokine, Telekine and Telepath categories. Specialised characters may only choose powers from one of these fields of psi-talent, as well as those in the General category.

Players who wish to fully comprehend all the nuances and effects of psi-talent are encouraged to read through the first few pages of the Magic chapter in *The Player's Handbook*, as many of the areas of effect, saving throws, and concentration checks used for psi-talent are very similar to those detailed for magic.

General

The powers in the General category are mainly those that almost any character with psi-talent can access, given time, practice and effort. They tend to be based on minor telepathic and precognitive abilities that come naturally to many psychics and while they lack the raw force of specialised powers, they tend to be more useful on a day-to-day basis.

Emulate Power
Level: 7
Manifestation Time: 1 action
Range: See text
Target, Effect, or Area: See text
Duration: See text
Saving Throw: See text
Power Resistance: See text
Power Points: 13 plus XP cost

Through the use of *emulate power*, a character may choose to manifest any other power, regardless of specialised category or whether he knows it, of 6th level or less. The effect of the manifested power is identical to its description in this book or the *Judge Dredd Rulebook*. However, this power draws a heavy price from the character.

XP Cost: 300 XP or the XP requirement of the emulated power, whichever is greater.

Gestalt
Level: 5
Manifestation Time: 1 minute
Range: 10 feet
Target: Manifester and up to fifteen other psi-talented characters who also know *gestalt*
Duration: 1 round/level (D)
Saving Throw: None
Power Resistance: No
Power Points: 9

The character is able to join his mind with other psi-talented characters, creating a psychic force far more powerful than its individual components. All participants must know the *gestalt* power and be willing to join their

THE PSI JUDGE CONCENTRATES HER TELEPATHIC POWERS —

DROKK! I SEE IT NOW! WHAT A BIMBO I'VE BEEN!

minds. Once linked, all the power points of every participant flow into a collective pool, which is increased by 20% by the *gestalt* power. For example, if ten psi-talented characters could each contribute 20 power points, the total would actually be 240 power points. When any power is manifested by the *gestalt* group, one character is chosen as the 'prime manifester' by consent of the rest. Any member of the group acting as the prime manifester may manifest any power known by any other member, even if he personally does not know it.

The *gestalt* group receives a +1 bonus per member to the saving throw DC required to resist any of its manifested powers. In addition, the group also receives a +1 bonus per member when making saving throws against powers targeted at any of them. If the group takes any damage from a psi-power, the damage is shared between members as the group sees fit. If the group was to take 16 points of subdual damage from a *psi-lash* targeted at them, for example, the group could share 4 points of damage between 4 members, or one member could take all 16 points, as they wished.

Once linked, all members of a *gestalt* must remain within 10 feet of another member. Any member who, willingly or not, moves out of this range will leave the *gestalt* and have their power points automatically reduced to 0. When *gestalt* ends or is dismissed, any remaining power points in the collective pool are divided evenly between all remaining participants, rounding down. No participant can exceed their usual maximum of power points by this method.

Mental Shield
Level: 0
Manifestation Time: 1 action
Range: Personal
Target: Manifester
Duration: 1 round/level
Saving Throw: None
Power Resistance: No
Power Points: 1

By building up a psychic wall of incredible proportions, the character is able to resist repeated psychic attacks. The character gains Damage Reduction 1 per manifester level (a 13th level psi-judge, for example, would gain Damage Reduction 13) against all powers that normally ignore any Damage Reduction. This Damage Reduction may not be increased in any way and only applies to psi-powers that inflict damage in hit points.

ONE THING'S FOR SURE — SOMETHING'S GOING ON. AND I BETTER FIND OUT WHAT.

Negate Psi-Talent
Level: 3
Manifestation Time: 1 action
Range: Medium (100 ft. + 10 ft./level)
Target or Area: One psi-talented character, one object or a 30 ft.-radius burst
Duration: Instantaneous
Saving Throw: None
Power Resistance: No
Power Points: 5

Negate psi-talent can be used to either end ongoing powers manifested upon a creature or object, or end powers within an area of effect. A negated power ends as if its duration had expired, though *negate psi-talent* may not be used to undo the effects of a power with an instantaneous duration.

This power may be used in one of two ways. A targeted negation is aimed at a single object or character who is affected by another power. A Negation check is made against each power affecting the target, which is 1d20 +1 per negating manifester level, against a DC of 11 + the enemy manifester's level. A character will automatically pass any Negation check against a power he manifested himself.

Negate psi-talent may also be used against every power within a 30 ft. radius. A Negation check (with a –2 penalty) is made for every character within this radius who is the subject of one or more powers, starting with the power with the highest manifester level. If this is successful, then a Negation check may be made for the power with the next highest manifester level, and so on. Once a power is failed to be negated, *negate psi-talent* effectively ends for that one character, though others may still take advantage of it so long as they continue to make Negation checks. Any ongoing power within this area will also require a Negation check, as if it were a character. Ongoing powers whose area overlaps with *negate psi-talent* will also face a Negation check, but success will nullify their effects only within the *negate psi-talent* area.

Null Psi-Talent
Level: 6
Manifestation Time: 1 action
Range: 10 ft.
Area: A 10 ft.-radius emanation, centred on manifester
Duration: 10 minutes/level (D)
Saving Throw: None
Power Resistance: See text
Power Points: 11

Upon activating this power, an invisible barrier stretching out to 10 feet surrounds the manifesting character, making him and everything within this area almost impregnable to psi-talent. Any psi-talent or power that moves into this area is automatically suppressed, though not negated. A character under the effects of *thrall*, for example, would be free while within the *null psi-talent* area, but would fall under the power's influence as soon as he left. Any psychic entity entering the field will automatically be returned to its home dimension unless it has Power Resistance. In this case, the manifester must make a Manifester Level check (page 108 of the *Judge Dredd Rulebook*) against the psychic entity's Power Resistance to force it back to its home dimension.

Negate psi-talent has no effect on null psi-talent and two null *psi-talent powers* coming into each other's area have no effect.

Physical Adaptation
Level: 5
Manifestation Time: 1 action
Range: Personal
Target: Manifester
Duration: 1 hour/level (D)
Power Points: 9

Through an incredible skill of mind over body, the character can actually adapt his physiology, for short periods of time, to resist a specific extreme environment. He can adapt to being underwater, extremely cold, extremely hot or even being in a vacuum or other airless environment. The character will be able to breathe and move normally and take no damage from simply being within that environment. Any environment that deals more than one dice of damage per round (such as being immersed in lava) cannot be resisted by this power. In addition, attack forms cannot be resisted either – even if a character has adapted himself to survive in a fiery environment, a flamethrower will affect him normally.

Turn Psi-Power
Level: 7
Manifesting Time: 1 action
Range: Personal
Target: Manifester
Duration: Until completely expended or 10 minutes/level
Power Points: 13

While *turn psi-power* is in operation, any psi-power targeted against the character will be rebounded back onto the original manifester. Powers not targeting the character specifically (such as those with an area of effect) are not affected. When *turn psi-power* is manifested, the Games Master rolls 1d4+6. This is the amount of psi-power levels that are affected by the turning, with each power turned subtracting its level from this score. If a power subtracts this figure into negative numbers, *turn psi-power* automatically ends and the targeted power functions normally.

Sense Living
Level: 1
Manifestation Time: 1 action
Range: Close (25 ft. + 5 ft./2 levels)
Target: Manifester
Duration: 10 minutes/level
Power Points: 1

By tuning into the psychic footprint of all living creatures around him, the manifester can sense their precise location and movements. For the duration of *sense living*, the manifester temporarily gains the Blind-Fight feat when fighting against living creatures only.

Settle

Level: 2
Manifestation Time: 1 action
Range: Close (25 ft. + 5 ft./2 levels)
Target: One animal or beast
Duration: Instantaneous
Saving Throw: Will negates
Power Resistance: Yes
Power Points: 3

By focussing his mental strength into the thought processes of an animal or beast, the manifester is able to calm any aggressive behaviour and leave the creature docile. *Settle* may be used against any animal or beast with an Intelligence score of 2 or less, and a number of Hit Dice equal to or lower than the manifester's level. Upon failing its saving throw, the creature will automatically be calmed and will not launch any attacks unless provoked for a period of one hour.

Dimensional

The range of psi-powers featured here in the Dimensional category are capable of altering the very fabric of reality itself. Those who use these powers draw upon the energies of psychic entities and other dimensions far beyond the real world, and yet remain heedless of the danger they court in attempting control of powers never meant for human control.

Banish

Level: 6
Manifestation Time: 1 action
Range: Close (25 ft. + 5 ft./2 levels)
Targets: One or more psychic entities, no two of which can be more than 30 ft. apart
Duration: Instantaneous
Saving Throw: Will negates
Power Resistance: Yes
Power Points: 11

Marshalling his psi-talent, a character using *banish* can literally throw psychic entities back to their home dimension through force of will alone. Up to 2 Hit Dice per manifester level of psychic entities can be instantly banished back to their home dimension, if they fail their saving throw and any Power Resistance check, with each use of this power. However, *banish* may only ever be used in conjunction with a psi-focus (see p69). *Banish* will not function on psychic entities that have taken over a mortal host.

Decay

Level: 5
Manifestation Time: 1 action
Range: Touch
Target: Character or object touched
Duration: Until discharged
Saving Throw: None
Power Resistance: Yes
Power Points: 9

By channelling the forces that dwell in the darker dimensions, the character can literally cause flesh to wither and plastisteel to crumble, as if inflicted with disease, rot or extreme old age. Living creatures affected by this power will immediately lose 1d6 temporary points of Constitution, which are regained at a rate of one point per full day of rest. Inanimate objects are dealt 1d10 x1d10 points of damage, ignoring all Damage Reduction. However, if a Power Resistance check ever causes *decay* to fail, dark energy feedback from other dimensions will cause the manifester to lose 1d3 temporary points of Constitution, which are recovered as described above.

Detect Psychic Entity

Level: 0
Manifestation Time: 1 action
Range: 60 ft.
Area: Quarter circle emanating from manifester to the extreme of the range
Duration: Concentration, up to 1 minute/level
Saving Throw: None
Power Resistance: No
Power Points: 1

SHE HOLDS THE ROBE TO HER, TRYING TO PICK UP IMAGES —

AKBARR GARGARAX! AKBARR AKBARR!

DROKK!

NEXT PROG: FREEPLUMBER — OR GRAND WARLOCK?

Through the use of this power, the character can detect any psychic entity inside the area of effect, whether it is normally visible or not. The time the character spends concentrating yields an increasing amount of information.

1st round: The character can sense the presence or absence of psychic entities.

2nd round: The number of psychic entities found in the area, along with the strongest psychic entity's relative power (Hit Dice).

3rd round: The relative power and location of each psychic entity.

Aura Strength: The strength of a psi-talent's aura depends on the power's or manifester's level:

Aura Strength

Psychic Entity's Hit Dice	Aura Strength
1-2	Dim
3-6	Faint
7-12	Moderate
13-20+	Strong
Deity or major demonic presence	Overwhelming

Each round, the character can turn to detect for psychic entities in a new area. *Detect psychic entities* can penetrate barriers, but is blocked by 1 foot of stone, 1 inch of plastisteel plating, a thin sheet of lead, or 3 feet of wood or dirt.

Create Poltergeist

Level: 5
Manifestation Time: 1 minute
Range: Close (25 ft. + 5 ft./2 levels)

Effect: One poltergeist is created
Duration: Instantaneous
Saving Throw: None
Power Resistance: No
Power Points: 9

By drawing forth elements of sentient energies from other dimensions, the character is able to literally create a poltergeist (see Chapter 8 for full details) in the real world without courting the dangers involved in *summon psychic entity*. However, he has no control over the poltergeist and it will be free to attack any living creature within its range.

Dimensional Anchor

Level: 4
Manifestation Time: 1 action
Range: Medium (100 ft. + 10 ft./level)
Effect: Ray
Duration: 1 minute/level
Saving Throw: None
Power Resistance: Yes
Power Points: 7

Through the use of *dimensional anchor*, a character can utterly prevent any movement by the target between dimensions. A ranged attack must be made against an unwilling target but, once so affected, it will be trapped in its present dimension or the real world, as appropriate. No special ability possessed by psychic entities can break a *dimensional anchor* and it will also serve to halt the effects of any *banish*, *dismiss* or *psychoportation* (of any type) power.

Dismiss

Level: 4
Manifestation Time: 1 action
Range: Close (25 ft. + 5 ft./2 levels)
Target: One psychic entity
Duration: Instantaneous
Saving Throw: Will negates
Power Resistance: Yes
Power Points: 7

Dismiss is a weaker version of *banish* that is often the only option available to most psi-talented characters to combat psychic entities. The targeted psychic entity adds its Hit Dice as a bonus to its saving throw but also suffers a penalty equal to manifester level. If successful, this power instantly forces the psychic entity back to its home dimension. A psi-focus (see p69) is necessary in order to

be able to use *dismiss*. *Dismiss* will not function on psychic entities that have taken over a mortal host.

Ectoplasmic Attack

Level: 3
Manifestation Time: 1 full round
Range: Close (25 ft. + 5 ft./2 levels)
Effect: One target
Duration: Instantaneous
Saving Throw: Fort halves
Power Resistance: Yes
Power Points: 5

By conjuring ectoplasm, the by-product of the psi-flux, into the real world, the character can use the semi-solid substance as a potentially powerful projectile. One selected target is automatically dealt 1d6 points of damage per manifester level (maximum 10d6). Damage Reduction is applied as normal and a successful Fortitude save will halve the damage. However, the manifester will suffer 1 point of damage (ignoring saves and Damage Reduction) for every 1 rolled on the damage dice used in the attack.

Ectoplasmic Shield

Level: 1
Manifestation Time: 1 action
Range: Touch
Target: Character touched
Duration: 1 round/level (D)
Saving Throw: Will negates (harmless)
Power Resistance: Yes (harmless)
Power Points: 1

Drawing upon ectoplasmic energy from other dimensions, the character cloaks himself in a shield of otherworldly material that can resist many attacks with ease. The character touched (which may, of course, be the manifester himself) immediately gains Damage Reduction 10 but this may not be combined with any other type of armour.

Evil Eye

Level: 2
Manifestation Time: 1 action
Range: Close (25 ft. + 5 ft./2 levels)
Target: One character
Duration: Instantaneous
Saving Throw: Reflex negates
Power Resistance: Yes
Power Points: 3

By focussing his will upon another living creature, the manifester can open a tiny rent in the fabric of reality to allow a victim a brief glance into the terrors that exist in other dimensions. In order for *evil eye* to function, the manifester must make eye contact with his target, who must make a Reflex save to avert his gaze before the full horrors of other worlds are thrust into his mind. If the target fails his save, he will immediately lose 1 temporary point of Charisma. This is regained at the rate of 1 point per full day of rest.

Exorcise

Level: 8
Manifestation Time: 1 action
Range: Close (25 ft. + 5 ft./2 levels)
Targets: One or more psychic entities within range
Duration: Instantaneous
Saving Throw: None
Power Resistance: Yes
Power Points: 15

Closely related to the *banish* and *dismiss* powers, *exorcise* is one of the most powerful weapons available to a character who intends to battle psychic entities. Up to 4 Hit Dice per manifester level of psychic entities can be instantly banished back to their home dimension, if their Power Resistance is overcome, with each use of this power. No saving throw is permitted to avoid the effects of *exorcise* and it will even ignore any *dimensional anchor* in place. *Exorcise* must be used in conjunction with a psi-focus (see p69) and will function normally upon entities that have possessed a normal host (see p50).

Ghostly Whispers

Level: 0
Manifestation Time: 1 action
Range: Close (25 ft.+5 ft./2 levels)
Target: One character
Duration: 1 round/level
Saving Throw: Will negates
Power Resistance: Yes
Power Points: 1

The character opens a small but potent portal from the real world into other dimensions, channelling the cacophony of wailing psychic entities directly into the mind of a victim. The victim will be constantly plagued by the whispers of these entities, luring him with promises of power, threats of dire torment or simply filling his head with incoherent babble. The victim will suffer a –1 penalty to all skill checks and saving throws while *ghostly whispers* is in effect.

Group Psychoportation

Level: 9
Manifestation Time: 1 action
Range: Personal and touch
Target: Manifester, touched objects and touched willing characters weighing up to 100 lb./manifester level
Duration: Instantaneous
Saving Throw: None and Will negates (object)
Power Resistance: No and yes (object)
Power Points: 17

This power is identical to *psychoportation*, but it allows the manifester to transport not only himself through dimensions to appear anywhere in the real world, but a group of willing allies as well. Group psychoportation uses the same rules as psychoportation to gauge its accuracy and if a mishap occurs, all characters being transported will suffer damage.

Psychoportation

Level: 8
Manifestation Time: 1 action
Range: Personal and touch
Target: Manifester and touched objects or one touched willing character weighing up to 50 lb./manifester level
Duration: Instantaneous
Saving Throw: None and Will negates (object)
Power Resistance: No and yes (object)
Power Points: 15

Through the strength of his will alone, the character can tear a temporary rift in the real world and instantaneously walk through other dimensions to materialise elsewhere, effectively teleporting himself in an eye blink. Objects and willing characters weighing a total of 50 lb./ manifester level may also be brought along.

The character must have a strong mental image of the destination for *psychoportation* to be effective – the clearer this image, the more likely the *psychoportation* will be successful and accurate. The table below is used

to determine how successful the power is – note that range is not a factor when using *psychoportation*. A character may instantly travel to the other side of the world, as long as he is familiar with his destination.

Familiarity	On Target	Off Target	Similar Area	Mishap
Very familiar	01-97	98-99	100	-
Studied carefully	01-90	91-97	98-99	100
Seen casually	01-75	76-88	89-98	99-100
Viewed once	01-50	51-66	67-96	97-100
Description	01-25	26-38	39-92	93-100
False Destination	-	-	01-80	81-100

A very familiar location is one in which the manifester has spent a great deal of time. Studied locations are those a manifester knows well or has studied often (such as through *psi-scan*). Seen casually locations are those the manifester has been to more than once but has not spent much time in, while viewed once is a place the manifester has only been to or seen once. Description refers to a place the manifester has never seen but has heard about or has a map to. False destinations are those that simply do not exist – this column of the table is used when the manifester has been misled or ill informed about his destination.

If a character is on target with his *psychoportation*, he appears exactly where he intended. Those who veer off target will appear 1d10 x1d10% of the distance that was to be travelled. Manifesters who find themselves in a similar area will not appear at their intended location but in a place that is visually similar. If a mishap occurs, every character being transported by *psychoportation* will suffer 1d10 points of damage, ignoring any Damage Reduction, and must re-roll on the table again.

Screams of the Damned

Level: 7
Manifestation Time: 1 action
Range: 30 ft.
Area: 30 ft. Cone emanating from manifester
Duration: Concentration, up to 1 round/level
Saving Throw: Will negates
Power Resistance: Yes
Power Points: 13

Screams of the damned is a far more potent form of *ghostly whispers*. Unleashing the wailing cries of tormented entities in other dimensions, the character can fill a large area with baleful screams, curses and pleas that can overwhelm even the staunchest of minds. Any character in the area failing their saving through must flee in terror away from the manifester for 1d6 rounds, falling catatonic if they are prevented from doing so. Those who succeed in their saving throw will still be distracted by a thousand angry or scared voices, forcing a –2 penalty to all attack and damage rolls, skill checks and saving throws.

Second Sight

Level: 1
Manifestation Time: 1 action
Range: Personal
Target: Manifester
Duration: 1 round/level (D)
Saving Throw: Will negates (harmless)
Power Resistance: Yes (harmless)
Power Points: 1

By tuning his mind and peering into other dimensions, the character can meld his vision of this world and others simultaneously. While *second sight* is manifested, the character will be able to see invisible psychic entities as if they were normally visible.

Summon Psychic Entity

Level: 3
Manifestation Time: Varies
Effect: Varies
Duration: Varies
Saving Throw: None
Power Resistance: No
Power Points: Varies

An extremely dangerous power in the hands of those who toy with the forces of other dimensions, the misuse of *summon psychic entity* has caused the deaths of more psykers than any other. This power allows a character to bring psychic entities directly to the real world. The full rules on summoning such creatures are detailed in Chapter 5.

Undeath

Level: 1
Manifestation Time: 1 action
Range: Close (25 ft. + 5 ft./2 levels)
Target: One corpse/level
Duration: 1 hour/level
Saving Throw: None
Power Resistance: No
Power Points: 1

This power allows a character to imbue a corpse with a shadow of its former soul, allowing it to once more walk the Earth as a zombie, a shambling creature utterly under the control of the manifester's will. Up to one corpse per level of the manifester may be turned into a zombie with each use of this power, though the manifester may never have a total of more zombies under his control than his level, regardless of how many times *undeath* is used. The zombies will follow the manifester or follow simple orders, as is desired. The corpse must be mostly intact for a zombie to be created and must be of medium size or smaller. Zombies are detailed on p85.

Pre-Cog

It is speculated that pre-cognitive powers are actually closely allied to those of dimensionalists, because of the way the psi-flux is used to grant access to other dimensions and times to peer into the past and foretell the future. Both specialists, however, maintain that each is separate and distinct and no matter where the dreams and visions of pre-cogs ultimately come from, they have little to do with the actual manipulation of dimensions. A skilled pre-cog is a fearsome foe but a valued ally, as the best can actually see into the future with a good degree of accuracy and predict the best course of action in any circumstance. Psi-Division works hard to recruit a constant supply of pre-cogs in order to provide valued aid in the investigations of all divisions within the Justice Department.

Combat Precognition

Level: 1
Manifestation Time: 1 action
Range: Personal
Target: Manifester
Duration: 1 hour/level (D)
Saving Throw: None
Power Resistance: No
Power Points: 1

By altering perceptions, the character is able to project his mind a fraction of a second into the future, in order to better evade incoming blows and shots. For the duration of *combat precognition*, the character gains a +1 insight bonus to his Defence Value. This bonus does not apply if the character is caught flat-footed.

Combat Prescience

Level: 2
Manifestation Time: 1 action
Range: Personal
Target: Manifester

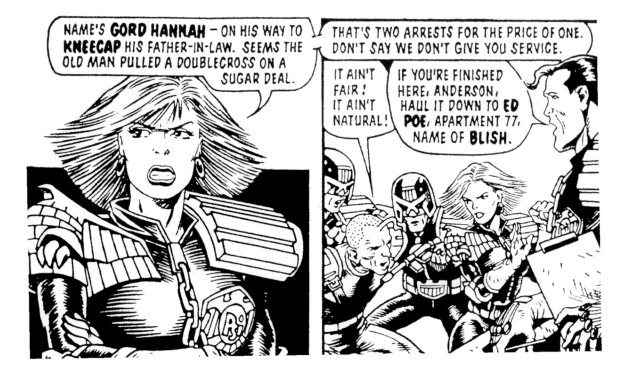

Duration: 1 minute/level (D)
Saving Throw: None
Power Resistance: No
Power Points: 3

Similar to *combat precognition*, combat prescience allows a character to extend his perceptions a few seconds into the future, allowing him to easily predict where to place his blows and shots in combat. For the duration of the power, the character gains a +2 insight bonus to all attack rolls.

Epiphany
Level: 9
Manifestation Time: 1 action
Range: Personal
Target: Manifester
Duration: Instantaneous
Saving Throw: None
Power Resistance: No
Power Points: 17, XP cost

The height of pre-cognitive powers, *epiphany* is attainable by very few psi-talented characters. By tapping into the ebb and flow of the psi-flux, the character can ask one specific question and receive a 'yes' or 'no' answer with 100% accuracy. This draws

upon a measure of the character's own life force and so is rarely used frivolously.

XP Cost: 500 XP

Foresight
Level: 8
Manifestation Time: 1 action
Range: Personal or touch
Target: See text
Duration: 10 minutes/level
Saving Throw: None or Will negates (see text)
Power Resistance: No or Yes (harmless)
Power Points: 15

Casting his mind into the immediate future, the character receives warnings of impending danger to either himself or the subject he touches. If he is about to be attacked from an unexpected direction, targeted by a psi-power or shot by an assassin, the character will know a fraction of a second before it actually happens and know how to best defend himself or the subject touched. He will therefore never be surprised or caught flat-footed while *foresight* is in effect. The power also grants a +2 insight bonus to Defence Value and Reflex saves. If the character touches another to gain the benefit of *foresight*, he will know when danger threatens the subject and the best course of action to take to avoid it, but the subject himself will not gain the insight bonus to Defence Value and Reflex saves.

Future Shock

Level: 1
Manifestation Time: 1 action
Range: Touch
Target: Creature touched
Duration: Until discharged
Saving Throw: None
Power Resistance: Yes
Power Points: 1

By focussing the glimpses of many different futures into another mind, the character can overwhelm a victim with disturbing images of their own injury and death, literally shocking their consciousness. Upon a successful melee attack, the character will deal 1d8 points of subdual damage, ignoring Damage Reduction.

Instant Precognition

Level: 4
Manifestation Time: 1 action
Range: Personal
Target: Manifester
Duration: Instantaneous
Saving Throw: None
Power Resistance: No
Power Points: 7

By casting his mind a split second into the future, the character is able to avoid some of the mishaps he would otherwise befall. *Instant precognition* may be used at any time as a free action, as if it were a quickened power, and will allow the character to re-roll any one attack roll, saving throw or skill check he fails.

Jinx

Level: 1
Manifestation Time: 1 action
Range: Close (25 ft. + 5 ft./2 levels)
Target: One character
Duration: 1 minute/level
Saving Throw: Will negates
Power Resistance: Yes
Power Points: 1

By gradually manipulating the strands of fate and viewing countless possible futures, the character is able to literally *jinx* an enemy and cause them to fight at a severe disadvantage. The victim of *jinx* suffers a –1

morale penalty to all attack rolls and skill checks they attempt while the power is in effect.

Precognitive Reflexes

Level: 0
Manifestation Time: 1 action
Range: Personal
Target: Manifester
Duration: Instantaneous
Saving Throw: None
Power Resistance: No
Power Points: 1

By casting his mind a split second into the future, the character is able to avoid some of the damage he would otherwise be dealt. *Precognitive reflexes* may be used at any time as a free action, as if it were a quickened power, and will allow the character to deduct one point of hit point damage he suffers from any source.

Psychic Compass

Level: 1
Manifestation Time: 1 action
Range: Personal
Target: Manifester
Duration: Instantaneous
Power Points: 1

Through the use of *psychic compass*, the character is able to instinctively know where he is and which direction north lies in. The information gained is general and takes the form of 'in the Cursed Earth approximately 35 miles east of the gates to Texas City' or 'one mile north of the Grand Hall of Justice.' Further movement by the character can cause him to lose his way once more, though subsequent uses of *psychic compass* will put him back on track.

Recall Injury

Level: 2
Manifestation Time: 1 action
Range: Medium (100 ft. + 10 ft./level)
Target: One living creature
Duration: Instantaneous
Saving Throw: Will halves
Power Resistance: Yes
Power Points: 3

By studying the fabric of time and finding the greatest sources of pain an enemy has ever endured, the character can send memories of wounds received in the past directly into another's mind, greatly magnified in effect. The victim of *recall injury* will suffer 3d6 points of subdual damage, ignoring Damage Reduction, though a successful Will save will halve this amount.

Psi-Scan Trap

Level: 6
Manifestation Time: 1 action
Range: Personal
Target: Manifester
Duration: 24 hours + 1 hour/level
Saving Throw: None
Power Resistance: No
Power Points: 11

Turning the powers of other pre-cogs against themselves, the character can prepare a trap for those who wish to spy upon his activities through the use of *clairvoyance*, *psi-scan* and other similar powers. Whenever another character with psi-talent attempts to observe him with such powers, both must make opposed Psi-Scanning checks, though the manifester of *psi-scan trap* gains a +10 insight bonus. If the observer succeeds in this check, his attempts to view the character proceed unhindered and without any knowledge on the part of the character. If the character succeeds in this check, not only is he undetected by the observer, but the observer also receives 4d4 points of damage (ignoring Damage Reduction) from potentially lethal psychic feedback.

Sequester

Level: 7
Manifestation Time: 1 action
Range: Touch
Target: One character or one object (up to a 2 ft. cube/level) touched
Duration: 1 day/level (D)
Saving Throw: Will negates (object)
Power Resistance: Yes (object)
Power Points: 13

The character has sufficient mental strength to actually manipulate the strands of fate and remove both creatures and objects from the prying sight of others. Any object or character under the effect of *sequester* becomes literally invisible to both psi-powers and normal sight (including mechanical and electronic means, such as robots or Tri-D cameras). Living creatures under the effect of *sequester* immediately become comatose and placed in a state of suspended animation until the power wears off. A Will save will prevent a character from

being *sequestered* – there is no saving throw to see a *sequestered* object or character.

Sixth Sense

Level: 3
Manifestation Time: 1 action
Range: Touch
Target: Character touched
Duration: 1 hour/level (D)
Saving Throw: Will negates (harmless)
Power Resistance: Yes (harmless)
Power Points: 5

By tuning a subject in to the immediate future, the character can allow the subject to automatically sense when he is threatened or in danger. This power temporarily grants the subject touched (which may be the manifester himself) the Sixth Sense feat, as described on page 45 of the *Judge Dredd Rulebook* for one hour per manifester level.

True Sight

Level: 5
Manifestation Time: 1 action
Range: Touch
Target: Character touched
Duration: 1 minute/level
Saving Throw: Will negates (harmless)
Power Resistance: Yes (harmless)
Power Points: 9

A character touched by *true sight* will immediately and automatically see things as they really are. They will see as normal in pitch darkness and will notice objects and characters hidden by psi-talent and powers. This includes seeing through all illusions, such as *fabricated reality* and astrally projected characters. The range of *true sight* is 120 feet. This power does not, however, grant the ability to see through objects and will not penetrate, for example, thick fog, nor will it detect creatures that are simply hidden out of sight. In addition, it cannot detect a character or object under the effects of *sequester*.

Pyrokine

Though true pyrokines are rare throughout the world, they are responsible for some of the most spectacular demonstrations of raw psi-talent. A good pyrokine is capable of exercising fine control of matter over energy, agitating particles so fires spontaneously ignite around him. With further practice, the pyrokine can learn how to actually manipulate fire and wield it as an offensive

weapon. A rogue pyrokine is always of great concern to Psi-Division, due to the damage they can cause and psi-judges are quickly dispatched to bring them in whenever located.

It is worth reviewing the fire rules on page 195 of the *Judge Dredd Rulebook* before using any pyrokinetic powers. Also keep in mind that fire damage ignores all Damage Reduction except against vehicles and robots.

Control Flames

Level: 2
Manifestation Time: 1 action
Range: Medium (100 ft. + 10 ft./level)
Area: One fire source up to small size
Duration: Concentration, up to 1 minute/level
Saving Throw: See text
Power Resistance: No
Power Points: 3

Through the use of this power, the character is able to manipulate and control any source of fire of small size or less. Fires of medium size or larger cannot be affected. The character may increase or decrease the size of the fire by one level each round – a tiny fire, for example, could be made into a small fire or be extinguished altogether. A

small fire could be made into a tiny fire or a medium-sized one. Fire can also be made to move from its fuel source at a speed of 10 feet per round and continue to burn until the duration of *control flames* expires. Fire being moved in this way may set light to other sources of fuel and may be used to attack a target, though it will be automatically extinguished if *control flames* expires and there is no fuel source in contact with it. The attack roll is made at the character's base attack bonus and will cause damage as usual for the size of fire. A creature being attacked by fire in this way must make a Reflex save to avoid catching alight as normal. The character manifesting *control flames* may switch his concentration from one fire to another throughout the duration of the power.

Fire of Retribution

Level: 5
Manifestation Time: 1 action
Range: Medium (100 ft. + 10 ft./level)
Area: Cylinder 10 ft. radius, 40 ft. high
Duration: Instantaneous
Saving Throw: Reflex halves
Power Resistance: Yes
Power Points: 9

So called because of the way it seems that Grud himself sends down a column of flame to immolate enemies of the character, *fire of retribution* generates a vertical column of fire that consumes anything in its area of effect. Any object within the area will suffer 1d6 points of fire damage per manifester level, up to a maximum of 15d6.

Flaming Shroud

Level: 6
Manifestation Time: 1 action
Range: Medium (100 ft. + 10 ft./level)
Target: One target of large size or smaller
Duration: Instantaneous
Saving Throw: Reflex negates
Power Resistance: Yes
Power Points: 11

One of the most spectacular uses of pyrokinetic power, *flaming shroud* allows the character to spontaneously create a sheet of green and blue fire that can smother a target of up to large size. If the target fails its Reflex save, it will immediately suffer 11d6 points of damage. The multi-hued flames automatically disappear after one round.

Flaming Weapon

Level: 2
Manifestation Time: 1 action
Range: Touch
Target: Melee weapon
Duration: 1 minute/level (D)
Saving Throw: None
Power Resistance: No
Power Points: 3

Flaming weapon allows the character to cause fire to erupt from the tip of any melee weapon he touches. The wielder of the weapon will not suffer any damage from the flames, but any target he successfully strikes with it will suffer 1d6 points of fire damage, in addition to the normal damage inflicted by the weapon. *Flaming weapon* does not cause any permanent damage to the weapon it is used upon, apart from some slight scorching.

Incendiary Rounds

Level: 7
Manifestation Time: 1 action
Range: Medium (100 ft. + 10 ft./level)
Effect: Up to 3 psychic incendiary rounds
Duration: Instantaneous
Saving Throw: None
Power Resistance: Yes
Power Points: 13

Through the use of this power, the character can psychically create up to three small bolts of fire that can be shot at any target before exploding. In all ways apart from range, these bolts are considered to be identical to the incendiary rounds carried in a Lawgiver and a ranged attack roll is made as normal to fire them at a target. If more than one *incendiary round* is created, then the ranged attack roll suffers rapid fire penalties as normal.

Incinerating Finger

Level: 0
Manifestation Time: 1 action
Range: Close (25 ft. + 5 ft./2 levels)
Effect: Ray
Duration: Instantaneous
Saving Throw: None
Power Resistance: Yes
Power Points: 1

The character can spontaneously ignite his own finger to create a small, candle-sized flame with which he can set light other objects. He may also use the flame offensively as a weapon, by causing it to shoot forward in a long jet of fire. Used in this way, a character must make a ranged attack against his target, which will be dealt 1d3 points of fire damage if struck.

Pyrokinesis

Level: 4
Manifestation Time: 1 action
Range: Long (400 ft. + 40 ft./level)
Target: One fire source
Duration: 2d6 rounds
Saving Throw: Reflex negates
Power Resistance: No
Power Points: 7

Pyrokinesis allows a character to turn an ordinary, existing fire into a burst of blinding pyrotechnics that can dazzle and harm any unfortunate enough to be nearby. The fire itself is unchanged by *pyrokinesis* but a series of bright flashes and loud noises will erupt from the flames for a period of 2d6 rounds. The actual effects of *pyrokinesis* depend on the size of the original fire, as detailed on the table below, but it will blind every creature within its area of effect (all opponents are considered to be in full concealment to the victim) while the victim himself will lose all Dexterity bonuses to Defence Value, move at half speed, allow attackers a +2

PSI-Powers

bonus on their attack rolls) and cause fire damage against any who are too close.

Size of Fire	Area of Effect (blinded)	Area of Effect (fire damage)	Fire Damage
Tiny	5 ft.	-	-
Small	10 ft.	-	-
Medium	20 ft.	5 ft.	1d6
Large	30 ft.	10 ft.	2d6
Huge	60 ft.	20 ft.	3d6
Gargantuan	100 ft.	30 ft.	4d6
Colossal	200 ft.	50 ft.	5d6

Pyrokinetic Burst

Level: 3
Manifestation Time: 1 action
Range: Long (400 ft. + 40 ft./level)
Area: 20 ft. radius
Duration: Instantaneous
Saving Throw: Reflex halves
Power Resistance: Yes
Power Points: 5

By agitating the molecules in air alone, the character can cause a ball of fire to spontaneously explode in the target area, immolating everything within. Every object within the target area will be dealt 1d6 points of fire damage per manifester level, up to a maximum of 10d6. The fire from *pyrokinetic burst* dissipates almost immediately, though smaller fires may remain if anything within the area catches light during this time.

Resist Flames

Level: 3
Manifestation Time: 1 action
Range: Personal
Target: Manifester
Duration: 1 minute/level
Saving Throw: None
Power Resistance: No
Power Points: 5

Through the use of resist flames, a character can become almost one with any fire source he comes into contact with. Flames will twist and lick around his body but never seem to actually touch or burn him. A character under the effects of *resist flames* will be immune to all fire damage for the duration of the power, regardless of their source. Note that this will not protect him against other heat-based attacks, such as lasers, as he only has the ability to keep fires and their effects from harming him.

Rolling Fire

Level: 8
Manifestation Time: 1 action
Range: Medium (100 ft. + 10 ft./level)
Effect: Cloud 30 ft. wide and 20 ft. high
Duration: 1 round/level
Saving Throw: Reflex halves
Power Resistance: No
Power Points: 15

Igniting the air within the area, the character causes a rolling cloud of flame to consume everything in its path. The cloud obscures all sight and will deal 4d6 points of damage to all objects within its area. The cloud will move 10 feet per round in any direction specified by the character, though strong winds will blow it out of control in their own direction.

Searing Metal

Level: 1
Manifestation Time: 1 action
Range: Close (25 ft. + 5 ft./2 levels)
Target: One metal object of small size or smaller
Duration: 1 round/level
Saving Throw: Reflex negates (see text)
Power Resistance: No
Power Points: 1

A minor but highly useful pyrokinetic power, *searing metal* allows a character to psychically heat any metal object so that it becomes almost too hot to hold. Only metal objects of small size or smaller can be affected by this power. Heated metal objects will automatically cause 1 point of damage per round (ignoring Damage Reduction) to= any character who holds them, though they may make a Reflex saving throw in order to drop the object in time to avoid this damage.

Sheet of Flame

Level: 1
Manifestation Time: 1 action
Range: 10 ft.
Area: Semicircular burst of flames 10 ft. long
Duration: Instantaneous
Saving Throw: Reflex halves
Power Resistance: Yes
Power Points: 1

A more powerful version of *flaming finger*, this power allows a character to project a thin sheet of flame in a semicircular pattern in front of him. Any creature or object within this area will suffer 1d4 points of fire damage per manifester level (up to

a maximum of 5d4), though a successful Reflex save will halve this damage. Any flammable objects in the area will also catch fire.

Spontaneous Combustion

Level: 9
Manifestation Time: 1 minute
Range: Long (400 ft. + 40 ft./level)
Target: One character or object
Duration: Instantaneous
Saving Throw: Fort negates
Power Resistance: Yes
Power Points: 17

PSI-Powers

Through the use of this extremely dangerous power, the character can cause any object or creature of any size to spontaneously ignite and begin to burn. The fire size will automatically be of the same size as the creature or object igniting, who will be dealt double the usual amount of damage every round due to the intensity of the flames. The flames cannot be extinguished unless the *spontaneous combustion* is somehow psychically negated, as the fire is burning from the inside of the target outwards. However, if the fire spreads to other areas, these can be extinguished as normal.

Tempest of Fire

Level: 8
Manifestation Time: 1 round
Range: Medium (100 ft. + 10 ft./level)
Area: 10 ft. radius/level
Duration: Instantaneous
Saving Throw: Reflex halves
Power Resistance: Yes
Power Points: 15

Tempest of fire allows the character to flood an entire area with a howling storm of ravaging flame that will incinerate anything in its area. Everything within the area of effect will take 1d6 points of fire damage per manifester level, up to a maximum of 20d6, making *tempest of fire* an extremely potent power.

Telekine

The ability to influence the world through the power of mind over matter is a goal for many individuals who possess psi-talent, though few are able to truly master the practice. A telekinetic specialist is capable of physically manipulating objects and particles by will alone, and the greatest can knock an enemy flat or pick up and throw large vehicles with a mere thought.

Aggrokinesis

Level: 6
Manifestation Time: 1 action
Range: Medium (100 ft. + 10 ft./level)
Target: One character or object
Duration: Instantaneous
Saving Throw: Fortitude halves
Power Resistance: Yes
Power Points: 11

Through the power of telekinesis, the character is able to literally rip a target apart into its component atoms. The victim of *aggrokinesis* will suffer 10d6 points of damage, ignoring Damage Reduction, as tiny particles of its body or structure are torn off and scattered about the surrounding area. A successful Fortitude save will halve this damage. If a character or object is reduced to 0 hit points through the use of *aggrokinesis*, it will be completely destroyed, leaving behind only a thin haze of dust.

Crushing Force

Level: 9
Manifestation Time: 1 action
Range: Close (25 ft. + 5 ft./2 levels)
Target: One character/round
Duration: Concentration, up to 4 rounds
Saving Throw: Fort negates
Power Resistance: Yes
Power Points: 17

Bringing his full telekinetic force to bear, the character is able to literally crush the life out of any living creature. For every round of concentration, the character can automatically kill one creature by crushing force. Only a successful Fortitude saving throw or Power Resistance can prevent this happening.

Concussion

Level: 2
Manifestation Time: 1 action
Range: Medium (100 ft. + 10 ft./level)
Target: One character or object
Duration: Instantaneous
Saving Throw: Fortitude halves
Power Resistance: Yes
Power Points: 3

By manipulating fine air particles to do his bidding, the character can literally pummel an object with pure telekinetic force. A target affected by *concussion* will sustain 3d6 points of damage, ignoring any Damage Reduction. The manifesting character may choose for this damage to be subdual damage, if he so desires. Targets behind cover will gain no protection against *concussion*, but they must be visible for the character to be affected. A successful Fortitude save will halve the amount of damage sustained.

Concussive Blast

Level: 5
Manifestation Time: 1 action
Range: Medium (100 ft. + 10 ft./level)
Target: One character or object

Duration: Instantaneous
Saving Throw: Fortitude halves
Power Resistance: Yes
Power Points: 9

A vastly enhanced form of *concussion*, *concussive blast* slams a target with awesome telekinetic power. A target affected by *concussive blast* will sustain 8d6 points of damage, ignoring any Damage Reduction. Targets behind cover will gain no protection against *concussive blast* but they must be visible to the character to be affected. A successful Fortitude save will halve the amount of damage sustained.

Control Body

Level: 2
Manifestation Time: 1 action
Range: Medium (100 ft. + 10 ft./level)
Target: One character of Medium size or smaller
Duration: Concentration, up to 1 minute/level
Saving Throw: Will negates
Power Resistance: Yes
Power Points: 3

The character can take over the body of another living creature and force it to perform actions of his bidding. This is not mind control in any shape or form – the character is exerting telekinetic will to literally move the victim's body and limbs as desired. The effects of *control body* are, however, limited and only body and limbs may be moved, as things like vocal chords are too fine to be manipulated with this power. The victim can be forced to walk, stand, sit, turn around and so on. It may also be forced into combat under the direction of the manifesting character. Its attack bonus will be equal to the character's base attack bonus, plus the victim's Strength modifier (or Dexterity modifier for ranged attacks), with a –4 circumstance penalty. The victim's Defence Value gets no bonus from its Reflex save. Instead, its Defence Value is equal to 10 + half the manifesting character's Reflex save, rounding down. The victim may make a Will save every round to break free of *control body*. In addition, any psi-talent may be manifested though a Concentration check must be made at DC 10 + the level of the power being attempted.

Greater Telekinesis

Level: 7
Manifestation Time: 1 action
Range: Long (400 ft. + 40 ft./level)
Target: See text
Duration: Concentration, up to 1 minute/level, or instantaneous (see text)
Saving Throw: Fort negates
Power Resistance: Yes
Power Points: 13

This power is identical to *telekinesis* but the character may move objects or characters weighing 100 lb. per manifester level. In addition, such objects will move 50 feet per round and creatures thrown violently will take 5d6 points of damage, as if they had fallen 50 feet.

Headjam

Level: 8
Manifestation Time: 1 action
Range: Close (25 ft. + 5 ft./2 levels)
Target: One character
Duration: Instantaneous
Saving Throw: Will negates
Power Resistance: Yes
Power Points: 15

By agitating the atoms within a victim's brain, the character can literally cause a head to explode like an over-ripe melon, slaying an enemy instantly. A victim of *headjam* must make a Will save or be instantly killed as his head explodes. Any object within 10 feet of the victim will suffer 1d6 points of damage as shards of bone and brain tissue are thrown outward with considerable force. Damage Reduction for this will apply normally. If the Will save is successfully passed, the victim will suffer no ill effects.

Levitate

Level: 2
Manifestation Time: 1 action
Range: Personal or close (25 ft. + 5 ft./2 levels)
Target: Manifester or one willing creature or one object (total weight up to 100 lb./level)
Duration: 10 minutes/level (D)
Saving Throw: None

Power Resistance: No
Power Points: 3

This power allows a character to move himself, another creature or an object up and down with but a thought. If *levitate* is to be used on another creature, they must be willing, and when used upon an object, it must be either unattended or held by a willing creature. Levitate will allow a character or object to move up or down 20 feet each round, as the manifester desires. No horizontal movement is permitted. In addition, levitating creatures will find it easy to unbalance themselves if they engage in combat. Their first attack roll will suffer a –1 penalty, their second –2, and so on, up to a maximum of –5. If the creature spends a full round stabilising itself, this penalty will drop to –1 again.

Lightning Catch

Level: 1
Manifestation Time: See text
Range: Close (25 ft. + 5 ft./2 levels)
Targets: Any free-falling objects or creatures in a 10 ft. radius whose weight does not total more than 300 lb./level
Duration: Until landing or 1 round/level
Saving Throw: Will negates (object)
Power Resistance: Yes (object)
Power Points: 1

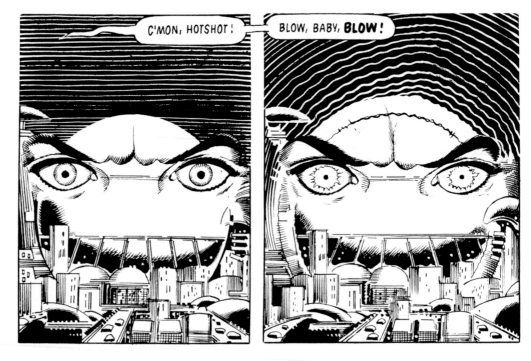

Through the use of this power, the character can telekinetically slow the descent of free-falling creatures or objects so no damage is caused when they land. Their rate of descent is changed to 60 feet per round, the equivalent of falling just a few short feet. However, when *lightning catch* expires, their normal rate of descent resumes. A character can manifest this power instantly, as a free action, if he himself is falling.

Magnify Force
Level: 1
Manifestation Time: 1 action
Range: Personal
Target: Manifester
Duration: 1 round/level
Saving Throw: None
Power Resistance: No
Power Points: 1

By channelling his telekinetic energy into each strike, the character can grant his blows in melee combat a greatly magnified force, allowing him to smash through almost any defences and cause a huge amount of damage. He gains a +10 bonus to all damage rolls made in melee combat and a +4 bonus to the AP of any melee weapon he wields for the duration of *magnify force*.

Mass Concussion
Level: 4
Manifestation Time: 1 action
Range: Long (400 ft. + 40 ft./level)
Area: 20 ft. radius sphere
Duration: Instantaneous
Saving Throw: None
Power Resistance: Yes
Power Points: 7

Similar to *concussion*, *mass concussion* is far more destructive and can affect a greater number of targets. All characters and objects within the area of effect will suffer 7d4 points of damage, ignoring any Damage Reduction.

Minor Telekinesis
Level: 0
Manifestation Time: 1 action
Range: Close (25 ft. + 5 ft./2 levels)
Target: See text
Duration: Concentration, up to 1 round/level, or instantaneous (see text)
Saving Throw: Fort negates

Power Resistance: Yes
Power Points: 1

This power is identical to *telekinesis* but the character may only move objects or characters weighing 1 lb. per manifester level. In addition, the range of *minor telekinesis* is greatly decreased.

Psychokinetic Shield
Level: 3
Manifestation Time: 1 action
Range: Personal
Target: Manifester
Duration: 1 hour/level (D)
Saving Throw: Will negates (harmless)
Power Resistance: Yes (harmless)
Power Points: 5

By surrounding himself with an invisible but toughened telekinetic shield, the character can literally walk through a hail of bullets or laser pulses without any harm coming to him. When manifested, *psychokinetic shield* grants the character 20 + 2d10 temporary hit points. Any damage suffered from a physical attack is deducted from these hit points first before the character himself loses any. The hit points of *psychokinetic shield* do not have any Damage Reduction and may not be regenerated in any way. The power expires as soon as the duration is reached, or when its hit points have been reduced to 0.

Telekinesis
Level: 4
Manifestation Time: 1 action
Range: Long (400 ft. + 40 ft./level)
Target: See text
Duration: Concentration, up to 1 round/level, or instantaneous (see text)
Saving Throw: Fort negates
Power Resistance: Yes
Power Points: 7

The character is able to move both objects and living creatures by the power of his mind alone. He can use *telekinesis* to provide a gentle and sustained pushing motion, or a short, violent thrust. A sustained push will move an object or creature weighing up to 25 lb. per manifester level 20 feet per round. If unwilling, a creature can negate this movement through a successful Fortitude save or Power Resistance. The object can be moved in any direction but may not be moved beyond the range of *telekinesis*. Any object can be manipulated with *telekinesis* as if the manifester was using just one hand –

so, buttons may be pressed, levers pulled and objects rotated in mid-air.

If the character decides to move objects with a short and violent force, he can direct them against any other target within 10 feet of their starting position. A total of 25 lb. per manifester level can be hurled in this way. If an object is thrown against a target, an attack roll is made using the manifester's base attack bonus, plus his Intelligence bonus. Non-lethal objects, such as crates, will cause 1 point of damage or every 25 lb. they weigh. Others, such as chunks of plastisteel, may cause up to 1d6 points per 25 lb. at the discretion of the Games Master. Damage Reduction applies as normal. Creatures hurled by *telekinesis* will take 1d6 points of damage when they strike a solid object, as if they had fallen 10 feet.

Telepath

The powers of a specialist telepath are considered by many psi-talented citizens to be the most powerful of any discipline. A skilled telepath can dominate the mind of another, reduce another psyker to a gibbering wreck or infiltrate dreams themselves. Much of a telepath's art is hidden and their powers do not have the flashy side effects of pyrokinetic or telekinetic displays. Instead, the mind itself is their domain and with their ability to manipulate almost any person they meet, the road to power beckons for those unscrupulous enough to use it for personal gain.

Attraction & Aversion

Level: 1
Manifestation Time: 1 action
Range: Close (25 ft. + 5 ft./2 levels)
Target: One character
Duration: 1 hour/level
Saving Throw: Will negates
Power Resistance: Yes
Power Points: 1

Through the use of this power, the character can plant a powerful attraction or aversion (manifester's choice of which) in the mind of any living creature. This attraction or aversion can be toward a specified person, place, action, object or event. The victim will take all reasonable steps to either get close to or stay away from the subject of the implanted attraction or aversion, as appropriate, though they will not perform any life-threatening actions to do so. If the character makes

himself the object of attraction, he gains a +4 bonus to his Charisma modifier when dealing with the victim.

Bind

Level: 2
Manifestation Time: 1 action
Range: Medium (100 ft. + 10 ft./level)
Target: One character of Medium-size or smaller
Duration: 1 round/level (D)
Saving Throw: Will negates
Power Resistance: Yes
Power Points: 3

By forcing his will into the mind of another, the character can separate a victim's higher brain functions from their body, effectively paralysing them. A victim of *bind* cannot move or take any actions, though they can defend themselves normally if attacked. They will also be unable to use any psi-talent.

Brain Drain

Level: 5
Manifestation Time: 1 action
Range: Touch
Target: Character touched
Duration: Until discharged
Saving Throw: Will negates
Power Resistance: Yes
Power Points: 1

By making physical contact with a victim, the character can drain their very life force, possibly rendering them helpless or, if used repeatedly, killing them outright. Upon a successful melee attack, the character will cause the victim 1d6 points of temporary Charisma or Intelligence damage (manifester's choice of which). A victim reduced to 0 Charisma or Intelligence will be slain. These points will be regained at the rate of 1 point for every full day of rest.

Confidante

Level: 9
Duration: Instantaneous
Power Points: 17, XP cost

Confidante is identical to *mindlink* except the telepathic bond forged between the two characters is permanent. In addition, a character may only have one *confidante* at any one time.

XP Cost: 2,000 XP

Domination

Level: 4
Manifestation Time: 1 action
Range: Medium (100 ft. + 10 ft./level)
Target: One character of Medium-size or smaller
Duration: 1 day/level
Saving Throw: Will negates
Power Resistance: Yes
Power Points: 7

Through the use of *domination*, the character is able to utterly control the actions of another. Once the telepathic link has been forged, the character can command his victim to perform virtually any action, so long as they share a common language. If no language is shared, only basic commands may be given (such as 'come here', 'fight him', etc.). Victims forced to perform actions that go against their basic natures (such as forcing a judge to murder an innocent citizen) may take a new saving throw for every such action, with a bonus of +1 to +4, as deemed suitable by the Games Master. Self-destructive orders are never carried out. The character need not see his victim in order to be able to exercise this control and the range, once the link is forged, is unlimited.

Doppelganger

Level: 6
Manifestation Time: 1 action
Range: Personal
Target: Manifester
Duration: 1 hour/level
Saving Throw: Will negates (see text)
Power Resistance: No
Power Points: 11

By infiltrating the minds of every-one close to him, the character may assume the appearance of someone else. This is not an actual physical change, but a telepathic command sent to all sentient creatures who view the character, convincing them that they are actually seeing someone else. The character can modify his clothes, physique and features however he wishes, though he cannot change his size more than a foot shorter, taller, thinner or wider. Every creature looking upon the character receives a Will saving throw to see through this illusion, with a cumulative +1 bonus for every other creature viewing the character, as the telepathic strain of keeping so many minds occupied becomes increasingly harder to keep up. Once one creature sees through *doppelganger*, the power ends.

Empathic Transfer

Level: 1
Manifestation Time: 1 action
Range: Touch
Target: Character touched
Duration: Instantaneous
Saving Throw: None
Power Resistance: Yes (harmless)
Power Points: 1

Through the use of advanced empathy, a sub-category of telepathy, the character can transfer wounds, poisons and diseases from one who is suffering to himself. Up to 8 points of damage per manifester level can be removed from a subject creature and placed upon the character with *empathic transfer* – effectively, the subject is healed 8 hit points per level while the character suffers the same amount. A poison, disease or radiation infection can also be transferred with *empathic transfer*. Last of all, the character can also choose to transfer one temporary ability point of damage per manifester level in the same way.

Enrapture

Level: 1
Manifestation Time: 1 action
Range: Close (25 ft. + 5 ft./2 levels)
Target: One person
Duration: 1 hour/level
Saving Throw: Will negates
Power Resistance: Yes
Power Points: 1

The use of *enrapture* allows the character to infiltrate the mind of another and convince them he is their trusted ally and friend. If the victim is currently being attacked by the character or his allies, they will gain a +5 bonus to their saving throw. *Enrapture* does not make the victim an automaton who will mindlessly obey instructions, but any actions or requests made by the character will be seen in the most favourable light possible. The victim will not do anything obviously suicidal and any harmful action made against him by the character or his friends will automatically break the power.

Fabricated Reality

Level: 3
Manifestation Time: 10 minutes
Range: Long (400 ft. + 40 ft./level)
Target: One character
Duration: Concentration, up to 1 minute/level (D)
Saving Throw: Will negates

Power Resistance: Yes
Power Points: 5

The character is able to fool the senses of a victim, tricking them into thinking they can see, hear, smell, taste or feel something that does not exist. For example, a judge could be made to look like an ordinary citizen, a stationary mo-pad look as if it were moving, a fresh munce burger look like it is rotten or a sunny day seem like it is overcast and raining. Nothing can be made invisible or seem to disappear with *fabricated reality*, though its appearance and nature may be changed.

Fatal Attraction

Level: 4
Manifestation Time: 1 action
Range: Medium (100 ft. + 10 ft./level)
Target: One character
Duration: Instantaneous
Saving Throw: Fortitude negates
Power Resistance: Yes
Power Points: 7

By implanting a deep-rooted and hidden death wish inside a victim's mind, the character can cause them to gradually become suicidal. The death wish takes 1d4 days to germinate and come forward to the conscious mind, during which time friends of the victim may make a Wisdom check at DC 15 each day to notice he is becoming increasingly fatalistic. Once 1d4 days have elapsed, the victim will seek to end his life by the quickest and most expedient means possible. If he attempts to end his own life but fails, another saving throw against *fatal attraction* may be made. If this fails, the death wish will take another 1d4 days to surface, with the same results as before.

Flense

Level: 7
Manifestation Time: 1 action
Range: Close (25 ft. + 5 ft./2 levels)
Target: One psi-talented character
Duration: Instantaneous
Saving Throw: Will negates
Power Resistance: Yes
Power Points: 13

By launching a direct mental assault upon another psi-talented character, the manifester can strip away their unique gift, potentially crippling them psychically. If the victim fails his saving throw, he will automatically lose one random psi-power of 6th level or less. This power

will not be regained until the victim advances one character level. Repeated uses of *flense* will continue to strip away more powers until the victim has no more to lose. This power has no effect on characters who do not possess psi-talent.

Mass Domination

Level: 7
Targets: One character/level, no two of which can be more than 30 ft. apart
Power Points: 13

This power is identical to *domination*, except that more victims can be affected simultaneously. In addition, the

CONTROL TO UNITS ED POE! GOT ANOTHER REPORTED DEMONIC POSSESSION —

character need not share a common language with those he controls. Different orders may be given to different victims without penalty.

Mass Suggestion

Level: 6
Range: Medium (100 ft. + 10 ft./level)
Targets: One character/level, no two of which can be more than 30 ft. apart
Power Points: 11

This power is identical to *suggestion*, except that more victims can be affected simultaneously. The same *suggestion* will apply to all victims who fail their saving throw.

Mindlink

Level: 2
Manifestation Time: 1 action
Range: Close (25 ft. + 5 ft./2 levels)
Target: One character.
Duration: 10 minutes/level
Saving Throw: None
Power Resistance: No
Power Points: 3

The character is able to forge a temporary telepathic link with another person, who must have an Intelligence score of at least 6 and be a willing subject. From this point onwards, the two can communicate telepathically with each other over any distance, though the link will not function if the two are in different dimensions.

Mindwipe

Level: 4
Manifestation Time: 1 action
Range: Close (25 ft. + 5 ft./2 levels)
Target: One character
Duration: Instantaneous
Saving Throw: Fortitude negates
Power Resistance: Yes
Power Points: 7

Mindwipe is an invasive telepathic power that allows the character to literally destroy the memories of a victim. Upon failing the saving throw, the victim will automatically lose one character level for every two manifester levels, to a maximum of five. As well as losing all class features, experience points, feats, skills, hit points, etc; all memories gained during those levels will also be lost. If a victim is reduced to 0 or less

character levels, they will have lost their entire life experience and will effectively have to be re-educated as if they were an infant. These lost levels may return if the victim can make a second saving throw after a full day has passed. If this is also failed, the lost levels are permanent.

Pain

Level: 2
Manifestation Time: 1 action
Range: Long (400 ft. + 40 ft./level)
Target: One character
Duration: Concentration, up to 5 rounds
Saving Throw: Will negates
Power Resistance: Yes
Power Points: 3

By forcing his will into the mind of another living creature, the character can inflict agonising pain. 3d6 points of damage, ignoring any Damage Reduction, will be automatically inflicted every round that concentration is maintained.

Psychic Static

Level: 5
Manifestation Time: 1 action
Range: Personal
Area: 100 ft.-radius emanation centred on manifester
Duration: 1 minute/level
Saving Throw: Will negates (see text)
Power Resistance: Yes
Power Points: 9

By flooding the surrounding area with *psychic static*, the character can make it extremely difficult and time-consuming for other psykers to manifest their talent. All psi-talent activity within the area of effect will require twice as many points as usual to manifest, unless the victims can succeed in a saving throw for every power they attempt. In addition, every 1 action power will now take a full round to manifest, regardless of whether the saving throw is made or not.

Psychic Surgery

Level: 9
Manifestation Time: 1 hour
Range: Close (25 ft. + 5 ft./2 levels)
Target: One character
Duration: Instantaneous
Saving Throw: Will negates
Power Resistance: Yes
Power Points: 17

In many ways, *psychic surgery* is the epitome of any telepath's powers, for it allows a character to penetrate deep inside the mind of another and repair any damage they have sustained from psychic attacks. Psychic surgery may be used to restore any lost ability points or hit points lost to another power or psychic entity, and may also be used to remove any current *suggestion*, *enrapture*, *attraction*, *aversion*, or any similar compulsion that exists in the mind. Insanity caused by powers or psychic entities may also be cured, and any character levels lost to *mindwipe* restored. In effect, so long as a psi-power did not cause actual death, the effects of it can be reversed through *psychic surgery*.

Psychic Vampire
Level: 5
Manifestation Time: 1 action
Range: Touch
Target: Character touched
Duration: 1 round/level
Saving Throw: Fortitude negates
Power Resistance: Yes
Power Points: 9

Psychic vampire allows the character to literally suck the psychic energy from a psi-talented victim to himself, making himself stronger as his enemy grows weaker. Upon a successful melee attack, 2 power points/ manifester level are immediately drained from the victim and transferred to the character's total. The character cannot gain more power points than his maximum through this method. This power has no effect on victims without psi-talent or power points.

Secret World
Level: 8
Manifestation Time: 1 minute
Range: Close (25 ft. + 5 ft./2 levels)
Target: One character
Duration: Instantaneous
Saving Throw: Will negates
Power Resistance: Yes
Power Points: 15

By penetrating far into a victim's mind and burrowing past any psychic defences, the character is able to close down all sense of the real world. Instead, the victim perceives a new world born of his own imagination, either a glorious paradise or a terror-filled nightmare, depending on his personality. The victim will not realise this is not the real world and will continue to explore it. In reality, the victim falls catatonic and may not be

revived by any mundane means. This will continue until the victim dies of thirst or starvation. A second *secret world* manifested upon the victim will release him from this power, as will *psychic surgery*, though no other treatment is possible.

Suggestion
Level: 2
Manifestation Time: 1 action
Range: Close (25 ft. + 5 ft./2 levels)
Target: One character
Duration: 1 hour/level or until completed
Saving Throw: Will negates
Power Resistance: Yes
Power Points: 3

Through a strong telepathic command, the character is able to implant an extremely strong *suggestion* into the mind of a victim. The *suggestion* must be worded in a reasonable manner and is limited to only one sentence. The victim will not do anything obviously self-destructive (such as shoot itself), though suggestion may be used to convince a victim that a rad-pit is actually harmless or a speeding jugger will actually stop before it hits the victim. A very reasonable suggestion may cause the saving throw against it to suffer a penalty, as determined by the Games Master – convincing a juve to stop mugging a harmless eldster may be such a circumstance. The *suggestion* lasts until the action is completed or until the power expires, whichever comes first.

Tailor Memory
Level: 4
Manifestation Time: 1 action
Range: Medium (100 ft. + 10 ft./level)
Target: One character
Duration: Instantaneous
Saving Throw: Will negates (see text)
Power Resistance: Yes
Power Points: 7

Another invasive telepathic power of great potential, *tailor memory* allows a character to insert a false memory of his own choosing directly into the mind of a victim. The new memory can be of up to 1 round in duration for every 4 manifester levels, and can have occurred at any time during the past week. To successfully tailor any memory, it is best to have an in-depth knowledge of the victim as any memory that is clearly out of place (such as a memory of an event occurring in Brit-Cit when the victim has never left Mega-City One) is likely to be rejected by the victim's mind. The Games Master may grant a +1 to +4 bonus to the victim's saving throw at his discretion if a memory is clearly out of place. Inserting memories that cannot possibly be true (such as having murdered a spouse when they are clearly present) automatically fail.

Thrall
Level: 9
Duration: Instantaneous
Power Points: 17, XP cost

This power is identical to *domination* except that the victim is permanently enslaved to the character's will if the saving throw is failed. In addition, if the victim is forced to carry out an order that goes against its basic nature (including self-destructive acts) then new saving throws are carried out with a –10 penalty. If this saving throw is successful, the action will not be carried out but the victim remains subject to *thrall*. Only another use of *thrall* with the intention of freeing the victim or *psychic surgery* can negate the effects of this power.

XP Cost: 5,000 XP

Xenoglossia
Level: 0
Manifestation Time: 1 action
Range: Personal
Target: Manifester
Duration: 1 hour/level
Saving Throw: Will negates
Power Resistance: Yes
Power Points: 1

Xenoglossia allows a character to telepathically communicate with any living creature with an Intelligence of 3 or more, regardless of language. Though the character will keep on speaking his own language, he will be understood by anyone who can hear him. At the same time, though others will also speak their own language, the character will be able to understand them fully. *Xenoglossia* does not permit a character to read or write in other languages, only communicate with those who speak them.

New Feats

This chapter greatly enhances and expands the range of psi and metapsi feats available to psi-talented characters in the Judge Dredd Roleplaying game. They are selected in the same manner as for any other feat though players should be aware that some of those detailed here have some very stringent prerequisites, requiring a character to be a specialist or be capable of manifesting very high level powers. With careful study and diligence, however, the right selection of feats can make any psi-talented characters very powerful indeed, enabling them to engage in hypnopathy, astral projection or simply make their existing powers overwhelming when unleashed upon an enemy.

Only characters who possess psi-talent may select psi or metapsi feats.

Additional Power (Psi)

The character learns one more power than is usual for a psi-talented character of his level.

Benefit: The character learns one additional power at any level up to one level lower than the highest-level power that he can manifest. This power must be a General power. However, specialists may choose to take an additional power in their category of specialisation. A specialist telepath, for example, could take an additional General or Telepathic power.
Special: A character may select this feat multiple times. Each time, he discovers a new power at any level up to one lower than the highest-level power he can manifest.

Astral Projection (Psi)

Through a process of deep meditation, the character is able to literally leave his body far behind and travel through the world as an astral projection, fully aware of his surroundings and yet invisible to other living creatures.

Prerequisites: Manifest 5th level psi-powers, Meditation.
Benefit: Immediately after a period of meditation (see the Meditation feat) the character may, instead of taking bonus power points, project himself astrally. While his body remains comatose, his mind leaves physical confines to explore the world around him. The character can see and hear normally through his astral projection and can move any solid object except lead and psychically-shielded materials at will. The astral projection has a speed score of fly 60 feet and is considered to be completely invisible to all creatures except psychic entities and those using *second sight* or *true sight*. While astrally projecting, the character is completely unaware as to what is happening to his physical body, even if it is under attack. A character may astrally project for a maximum of 10 minutes x his Charisma modifier.

Change Instruction (Psi)

The character can change and modify a psychic entity's instructions in his service after summoning it.

Prerequisites: *Summon psychic entity*, specialist (dimensionalist).
Benefit: A controlled psychic entity may be given new instructions at any point of its service. This is a full-round action and may only be attempted upon a psychic entity the character has personally summoned and controlled. To succeed, an Instruction check must be made at DC 10 + the psychic entity's Hit Dice. The character's Charisma modifier is used as a modifier to this roll. If successful, the character may give the psychic entity a new instruction following the usual rules. Note that once any instruction is complete, the psychic entity will immediately return to its home dimension. This feat may not be used to extend the time the psychic entity remains in the material world.

Defensive Block (Psi)

The character is adept at blocking powers from a particular specialisation.

Prerequisite: Specialist Focus in the specialisation chosen.
Benefit: Upon gaining this feat, the character immediately selects one specialisation he has Specialist Focus in. The character now gains a +2 to all saving throws against powers of the chosen specialisation.

Drain Psi-Talent (Psi)

While attacking a psi-talented enemy with psychic powers, the character can potentially cripple his target to prevent it retaliating.

Prerequisites: Mental Adversary.

Benefit: When attacking an enemy with psi-talent, the character can also drain his Charisma modifier x 4 power points from his opponent. This feat may only be used when employing one of the following powers: *brain drain, flense, mind bomb, pain, psi-lash,* or *recall injury.* The power will cost an extra 3 points to manifest if it is boosted with Drain Psi-Talent.

Encompassing Power (Metapsi)

By feeding his powers with additional psychic energy, the character is able to greatly increase the effects of his manifestations.

Benefit: The character may double the area of effect of any power he manifests at an additional cost of +8 power points. Only powers listed as having an area of effect may be used in conjunction with this feat.

Enhanced Power (Metapsi)

The character is able to feed greater reserves of psychic energy into his manifestations, making them vastly more potent than before.

Benefit: All variable effects of an enhanced power (such as damage) are increased by one-half. An enhanced power will therefore deal half again as many hit points,

affect half again as many targets, and so on, as appropriate. Saving throws, Power Resistance and opposed checks are not affected. Powers without random variables are also not affected. An empowered power costs a number of power points equal to its standard cost +6.

Far Power (Metapsi)

The character is able to project his long-ranged powers over an incredible distance.

Benefit: The character may increase the range of any power noted as being long ranged in its description by 100 feet. This will increase the cost of the power by +3 power points. The range can be increased several times in this way by simply increasing the multiple of the cost. So, for example, a power increased in range by 100 feet will cost 3 extra power points, one increased by 200 feet will cost 9 extra power points, one increased by 300 feet will cost 18 extra power points, and so on.

Greater Specialist Focus (Psi)

The specialist powers manifested by the character are extremely potent and may only be resisted by victims of great endurance.

Prerequisites: Specialist Focus, Specialist (any).
Benefit: This feat is identical to Specialist Focus except the character adds +4 to the DC of any saving throw made against his manifested powers. Again, this bonus only applies to powers from his specialist area of psi-talent and does not stack with the bonus gained from Specialist Focus.

Hypnopathy (Metapsi)

The field of hynopathy is still a relatively new one in psychic abilities and is fully understood only by a small number of individuals. By forging a link with a sleeping subject, the character is able to enter their dreams and search through the subconscious mind directly, bypassing active and possibly hostile thoughts.

Prerequisites: Wis 13+, *mindlink*, specialist (telepath).
Benefit: The character may use *mindlink* on a sleeping subject. Once this has been achieved, the character can then go on to use any general or telepathic power upon the subject and automatically succeed in any Manifester check they are called to make in order to beat any

existing Power Resistance. In addition, the subject will automatically fail in any saving throw to resist the power. Hypnopathy is extremely draining to the character and may only be used once per day. Any number of powers may be used upon the subject but the duration of hypnopathy is limited to that of the *mindlink* used to enter the subconscious mind. While using hypnopathy, the power point cost of all powers, including the original *mindlink*, are doubled.

Improved Transformation (Psi)

The character can draw greater quantities of electricity to fuel his psi-talent, though this is not without risk.

Prerequisites: Transformation.
Benefit: Improved Transformation may only be used on larger power sources such as vehicles or generators, not power packs. This feat functions in the same way as Transformation except that the character will recharge 1d6 power points per round. However, if a 5 or 6 is rolled, the character will also sustain 1d6 points of damage, with no Damage Reduction possible.

Innate Power (Psi)

Having a staunch and disciplined mind, the character is capable of manifesting one power with next to no effort – all it takes is but a brief thought.

Prerequisites: Inner Strength, Talented.
Benefit: The character immediately choose any 0, 1st, 2nd, or 3rd level power he knows. From this point on, he can attempt to use that power without paying any power points. To use this power, the character must have as many power points as he would normally require to manifest it – he may not spend the power points, but he needs them in reserve. A Charisma check must then be made at DC 11 for a 0-level power, 13 for a 1st level, 15 for a 2nd level, and 17 for a 3rd level. If successful, the power is manifested normally with no power point cost. If failed, the power manifests normally, but the power points cost must be paid.
Special: This feat may be selected multiple times. Every time the feat is taken, a new power may be chosen to be used in conjunction with Innate Power.

Longevity (Psi)

The character has learnt to channel his psychic energy into his general physical well being. The years never seem to touch him and he will not age a day while his psi-talent remains.

Prerequisites: Manifest 6th level psi-powers.
Benefit: Once a character selects the Longevity feat, he will no longer age physically. However, this is draining to his psi-talent and he will permanently lose two power points per manifester level from his total power points. A 16th level psi-judge, for example, will have 83 power points at his disposal, not 115. Note that Longevity does not grant immortality – the character is still vulnerable to injury, poison, radiation and disease. He will, however, never grow physically older than his current age.

Magnify Power (Metapsi)

Drawing upon great psychic reserves, the character can magnify his powers so they are greatly increased in potency when manifested.

Benefit: The character is able to manifest powers as if they were of higher level than they truly are or he would normally be capable of. All effects that are dependant upon power level, such as saving throw DC, are assumed to be based on the new power level. Note that this does not increase the manifester level of the power, just the power's own level. This costs an additional number of power points equal to the new power being attained, as shown on the table below. No power may be increased to beyond 9th level.

New Power Level	Extra Power Points Required
1	1
2	3
3	5
4	7
5	9
6	11
7	13
8	15
9	17

Maintain Power (Metapsi)

Almost effortlessly, the character is able to maintain powers that normally require a great deal of concentration to manifest

Prerequisite: Inner Strength, Talented.
Benefit: The character can maintain a power that has a duration of Concentration subconsciously, allowing him to perform a greater range of actions while maintaining the power. Powers that require a full round or a standard action of concentration now only require a move-equivalent action to maintain. A power maintained in this way costs a number of power points equal to its standard cost +4. Powers cannot be maintained longer than a

number of rounds equal to its normal duration or one round per manifester level if a concentration duration is not specified. A character cannot maintain more than one power at a time in this way. He must still make Concentration checks to maintain the power as normal.

Meditation (Psi)
Through a series of well-rehearsed calming and meditation techniques, the character is able to settle and purify his mind in order to better utilise his psi-talent.

Prerequisites: Manifest 3rd level psi-powers.
Benefit: Once per day, the character may meditate for a period of no less than one hour, during which time he must remain undisturbed and take no other action. After this meditation has been completed, the character will have his power points temporarily boosted by an additional 20% (rounding down) for a period of 24 hours. This will temporarily become his new maximum power point score for this duration only. A 15th level psi-judge after meditating, for example, will have not 100 power points, but 120.

Mental Adversary (Psi)
Against enemies who posses psi-talent, the character is utterly lethal, being capable of causing a great amount of damage with every psychic attack he makes.

Prerequisites: Cha 13+.
Benefit: When attacking an enemy with psi-talent, the character can choose to deal additional damage above and beyond what he would normally be capable of. This feat may only be used when employing one of the following powers: *mind bomb, pain, psi-lash,* or *recall injury*. The power will cost an extra 3 points to manifest if it is boosted with Mental Adversary but, if the attack is successful, will cause an additional amount of damage equal to the character's manifester level.

Mental Snare (Psi)
When attacked by an enemy possessing psi-talent, the character is able to draw his foe's mental energies forward into a cunningly prepared mind snare, draining power as he does so.

Prerequisites: *Mental shield, mind shield*.
Benefit: So long as he has either *mental shield* or *mind shield* currently manifested, the character may drain power points from any enemy who attacks him with a

damaging psi-power. Upon receiving damage (which may be hit points or ability damage) from a power, the character may immediately choose to expend 2d6 power points. If he does not have enough power points to cover this cost, Mental Snare automatically fails. If he does have the required power points, his enemy will automatically lose 10 + the character's Charisma modifier in power points.

Permanent Control (Psi)
The character is able to establish such overriding mental bonds over weaker psychic entities that they remain permanently under his control.

Prerequisites: Cha 15+, *summon psychic entity*, specialist (dimensionalist).
Benefit: After successfully controlling a psychic entity with 5 Hit Dice or less, the character may choose to permanently bring it under his will. From this point on, the psychic entity will be trapped in the material world and will be compelled to follow any of his instructions at any time. On the completion of any instruction, it will return to the character's side rather than disappearing back to its home dimension. Only one psychic entity may be under permanent control at any one time.
Special: A character may take this feat multiple times, allowing him to have more than one psychic entity under permanent control.

Precognitive Sense (Psi)
His mind always open to the vagaries of a myriad possible futures, the character has an awareness that goes far beyond ordinary and mundane senses.

Prerequisites: Manifest 4th level psi-powers, specialist (pre-cog).
Benefit: The character may manifest *detect psi-talent* as a free action and at no cost of power points. He may use this feat any number of times each day and the power will be treated as if being manifested at his current manifester level.

Quicken Summoning (Psi)
The character demonstrates an incredible ability to perform summonings faster than normal while maintaining a very low margin of error.

Prerequisites: Int 15+, *summon psychic entity*, specialist (dimensionalist).
Benefit: The time required to perform a summoning is halved with no penalty. A slow summoning will thus take the normal amount of time, while a hurried summoning will quarter it.

Specialist Focus (Psi)

A master of his chosen area of study, the character's manifestations of his specialist psi-talent are nigh on unstoppable.

Prerequisites: Specialist (any).
Benefit: The character adds +2 to the DC of any saving throw made against his manifested powers. However, this bonus only applies to powers from his specialist area of psi-talent – a telepath, for example, would gain this bonus to his telepath powers, not to his general powers.

Strength of Will (Psi)

The character possesses an incredibly strong will and is able to dominate many psychic entities with his thoughts.

Prerequisite: Iron Will, *summon psychic entity*.
Benefit: The character gains a permanent +2 circumstance bonus to all Control checks he is required to make.

Synergy (Psi)

The character's awareness increases as his links with the psi-flux grow, greatly boosting his talent. By becoming one with the psi-flux, he can tap its resources far more readily and is now able to use his powers with greater frequency.

Prerequisites: Manifest 4th level psi-powers.
Benefit: The character now has an increased power point recharge rate. He restores any power points he uses at a rate of two points per hour, or four points if he is resting or sleeping.

Telekinetic Punch (Psi)

Many telekinetic specialists are able to hold small reserves of their psi-talent in check, ready to be unleashed whenever they lash out at an enemy.

Prerequisites: Specialist (telekinetic).
Benefit: So long as the character has at least one power point available, he may use his psi-talent to increase the power of his unarmed blows. His fist attacks will cause 1d6 points of damage on a successful hit and will have an Armour Piercing score of 2. This attack still counts as an unarmed strike for the purposes of attacks of opportunity. Note that the use of this feat does not actually use any power points – the character just has to have at least one power point spare in order to utilise it.

Transformation (Psi)

The character possesses the unusual ability to draw upon raw electricity to fuel his psi-talent and can literally recharge himself with a suitable power source. The process is difficult to master and takes a great deal of concentration but ensures the character will rarely be lacking in psychic ability.

Prerequisites: Con 13+.
Benefit: By spending one full round in contact with a source of electricity, the character can regain power points at an accelerated rate. He may perform no other action while recharging in this way but will receive one power point per round while he does so. The character will completely drain a light power pack in one round, a medium power pack in two rounds and a heavy power pack in three. Larger sources of power (such as a vehicle or generator) will not be drained but the character can never gain more power points than his maximum in this way. Note that this feat does not grant any special immunity to electricity though the character need not necessarily expose himself directly to the current – just being in contact with the source of electricity is sufficient.
Special: This feat must be selected at first level during character creation. It may not be taken at a later time.

Twin Power (Metapsi)

Gathering his mental resources, the character can manifest powers extremely rapidly, in order to gain a greater chance of blasting through an enemy's mental defences.

Benefit: This feat allows a character to effectively manifest a power twice upon a target. Any variables in the power (such as damage) apply to both of the resulting powers. The target suffers all the effects of both powers individually and receives a saving throw for each. A twinned power costs a number of power points equal to its standard cost +8.

Summoning

The *summon psychic entity* power is an extremely dangerous tool in the hands of any but the most accomplished psi-talented characters. By drawing upon the very essence of other dimensions, psykers are capable of bringing psychic entities into the real world in order to fulfil their own diabolical schemes and plans. A rogue dimensionalist in a lowly street gang may be able to tip the balance in any rumble with a rival gang by calling forth cruel ghouls or entities to smite his enemies – but he will always run the risk of the psychic entities breaking free of his control and turning upon the mortal foolish enough to believe he could harness their power in the first place.

This chapter looks in detail at the ways a skilled dimensionalist (or dabbler in the dark arts) can utilise the power of psychic entities to achieve his greatest desires, as well as the dangers that are always present to those who mess with knowledge man was never meant to know. Always remember that there is no such thing as a bad dimensionalist – such citizens quickly succumb to the excesses of the art they vainly attempt to control.

Summoning Psychic Entities

Once a psyker learns the *summon psychic entity* power, bringing such fell creatures into the real world is, in theory, a simple exercise in will and mental fortitude. In practice, the psyker is putting himself directly in the path of some of the most powerful creatures ever to have walked this world and others. There is much that can go wrong and while many psychic entities forever seek a chance to enter the real

THROUGH HIS BLOOD WE WILL BE RELEASED !

THROUGH HIS DEATH WE WILL BE REBORN !

world and wreak havoc upon mankind, few are willing to do so at the behest and control of a mere mortal.

To bring a psychic entity into the real world, the psyker merely manifests *summon psychic entity* (which can take a great deal of time if he seeks to call a particularly powerful creature to his bidding). If successful, the entity will appear, drawn from another dimension. Now will begin the shortest part of the summoning, but also the most hazardous. The psyker must apply his own mental willpower to break the spirit of the psychic entity and bend it to his own demands. The successful application of this last process is the ultimate goal of all dimensionalists. Failure does not often grant one a second chance to correct mistakes.

It must be noted here that, contrary to popular beliefs and bar-room gossip, the sacrifice of animals or sentient beings is *never* required for the successful controlling of psychic entities. On the other hand, such offerings can greatly aid an evil dimensionalist with no remaining scruples and even the most accomplished will be hard pressed to control the greatest of the entityic powers without a valuable soul to offer in exchange for services...

The Risks

The summoning itself holds little danger for the psyker, other than the fear of discovery, for it tends to be a fairly lengthy process. Failure in summoning an entity from another dimension is likely to result only in the loss of mental strength and psychic reserves for no gain. The danger lies in the process of actually controlling an entity. Such beings do not enjoy being ripped from their homes in other dimensions and will be greatly enraged by the intrusion into their often incomprehensible plans and designs.

Upon the completion of a successful summoning, the psyker will be confronted by the entity he sought to call. Such an entity will be murderous in nature, its desire for cruelty and destruction magnified by the temerity of a mortal seeking to dominate it by his own mind. The psyker has but one chance to bring the creature under control. A single slip, just one break in concentration, will leave the entity free to roam the real world. Its first act will be to exact vengeance upon the summoner, either rending him limb from limb in an orgy of blood-letting, or carrying him off to its home dimension where he will suffer for an eternity as the plaything of its kin. Even if the psyker manages to somehow survive and escape such a baleful existence, he is unlikely to ever be. . . quite right again. Few dimensionalists are aware of the risks they run every time they attempt a summoning though horrific stories and tales abound of their predecessors. Most fervently pray for a quick end should they ever make a costly and fatal mistake at this most critical of times.

In rare cases, the psychic entity may seek to stay in the real world to wreak havoc for a little longer than the summoning ordinarily permits. In such circumstances, the psyker will be viciously assaulted physically, mentally and spiritually as the entity attempts to possess him, gaining absolute control of his functions and twisting his body beyond all recognition. Bones bend and snap, skin warps and muscle expands as the mortal body strains to contain the entityic energies it is subjected to. The chances of surviving such a fate are practically non-existent.

Summoning

To bring one of these creatures into the real world, a psyker merely has to manifest the *summon psychic entity* power. He may choose to bring any creature listed in Chapter 8 that is listed as being a 'psychic entity'. A ghoul, for example, could be summoned, as it is considered a true psychic entity, but a zombie could not.

A summonings takes as many hours to perform as the Hit Dice of the subject psychic entity. The summoning of a ghoul, for example, takes four hours. During this time, the psyker concentrates his mind, sending it soaring through other worlds and dimensions as he seeks to find the trail of the entity he wishes to summon. Once found, he must create mental bonds that will trap the entity and bring it, kicking and screaming, into the real world. Whilst performing the summoning, the psyker may take no other action and so cannot manifest any other powers.

Using *summon psychic entity* will drain a number of power points equal to the Hit Dice of the psychic entity being summoned, multiplied by five. Summoning a ghoul with 4 Hit Dice, for example, would use 20 power

Psi-Foci, Pentagrams and Their Uses

As with the study of psychic entities themselves, there are many misconceptions based around pentagrams and their use within the dark arts. It is a common belief, for example, that a pentagram exists to protect the psyker from the malevolent spirits that he calls upon for aid. It serves, however, a very different purpose.

To pull a being of any power from distant dimensions and make it manifest in the real world takes a tremendous amount of psychic energy, the type of which few mortals are able to withstand, let alone manipulate to their own ends. The pentagrams sometimes used in summoning are, quite simply, carefully constructed psi-foci designed to channel and magnify a psyker's own forces in order to build enough power during the summoning to call an entity into the real world. By focussing this much energy over a relatively short period of time, the power inherent within a psi-focus is completely expended when the summoning is complete, leaving the psyker with no protection against the creature he has just summoned other than his own knowledge and force of will.

Few psykers actually use pentagrams as psi-foci when attempting to call entities from other dimensions, for it is commonly regarded as an ancient and medieval practice now defunct with the application of the latest technologies. However, a few still follow the old ways and a correctly drawn pentagram is just as powerful a psi-focus as anything else in a character's psychic arsenal. Psi-foci are covered in more detail on p69.

points, regardless of whether the attempt was actually successful or not. If the psyker is disturbed during his summoning, he will lose the power points as normal, and the attempt will be automatically unsuccessful.

Once the power points have been spent and the time for summoning is complete, the character must make a Summoning check in order to physically bring the psychic entity into the real world.

The Summoning Check
The basic Summoning check is DC10 + the Hit Dice of the psychic entity.

Failure in the Summoning check results in nothing more than the expenditure of power points and the absence of said entity. Of all the checks used in summoning psychic entities, this is the one that is safest and least costly to fail in.

A successful Summoning check will draw the entity from its own dimension, forcing it to appear before the psyker. Now comes the most difficult part of the ritual – controlling the entity and making it subject to the character's will.

The Control Check
The basic Control check is DC 10 + twice the Hit Dice of the psychic entity.

If passed, the Control check will allow the summoner to give the entity instructions to be carried out, as detailed below. A failed roll will likely mean the psyker is in very serious trouble as the summoned entity frees itself of the bonds that have been placed upon it. It will immediately attack the psyker as described on p47.

For both Summoning and Control checks, a roll of a 1 is an automatic failure and a roll of 20 an automatic success.

Shifting the Odds

With his very life and soul at stake, any psyker will work hard to increase the chances of a successful summoning and control of the entity he calls. At the same time, however, other factors may intrude upon the summoning to make it far more difficult. The different bonuses and penalties that may be applied to Summoning and Control Checks are listed here.

Expertise

The experienced psyker will naturally be far more capable than one attempting to summon his very first entity. He will have the strength of will and purpose to cover minor mistakes and errors, becoming consistently successful in the practice. A psyker's total character levels are added as a bonus to every Summoning and Control check.

Study and Preparation

Summoning entities is not an art that can be easily mastered by those short of memory or failing in their mental faculties. It requires precise observation and recollection, for a mistake made in the preparation of a psi-focus or in the mental disciplines required to send a mind through other dimensions can cripple a summoning. A psyker's Intelligence modifier is added to every Summoning check.

Force of Will

It is often a psyker's sheer force of will and personality that can make the difference between success and failure when he comes to actually controlling an entity. A battle of titanic wills can erupt in a fraction of a second as the entity strains to break free of the bonds being imposed upon it, even as the psyker exerts his mind to bring it under control. A psyker's Charisma modifier is added to every Control check.

Slow Summonings

Psykers, by necessity, take great care in their preparations for the summoning. Given enough time, greater safeguards and mental defences can be employed, with every stage of the summoning being checked and re-checked for any possible mistakes. By doubling the time required to perform a summoning, a psyker will be granted a +2 bonus to both his Summoning and Control checks.

Hurried Summonings

By the same token, there may be times when a psyker will be put under the severest pressure to summon an entity as quickly as possible. Under such circumstances, it is almost inevitable that errors and mistakes will arise, making the whole process harder and a lot more dangerous. Hurrying a ritual will reduce the time required to perform it by half but will impose a –4 penalty to both Summoning and Control checks.

The Entity Controlled

Upon the successful summoning and control of an entity, the character will have the ability to command the creature to do his bidding. As with every other part of this practice, there are rules that must be obeyed.

A controlled entity is compelled to carry out and complete a single, nine-word instruction issued by the summoner for a duration of no more than one hour. Once the instruction has been carried out or an hour has elapsed, whichever comes first, the entity instantly winks out of existence in the real world and is immediately returned to its home dimension.

This instruction *must* be given at the moment of control, straight after the entity has been summoned or it will merely return to its dimension. Instructions cannot be issued after this time, no matter now powerful the psyker is.

Anything may be demanded and the entity is compelled to carry out such instructions to the best of its ability. A character may ask the entity, for example, to act as a bodyguard, or to assassinate an enemy. Many entities have existed since before the dawn of time and are thus incredible sources of long-forgotten knowledge. Others, such as ghosts, excel as spies. These are just a few of the most basic examples of what a character may compel an entity to do. In practice, he is limited only be the entity's powers and his own imagination.

Multiple Instructions

Passing the Control check when the entity is summoned allows the psyker to issue a single, nine-word instruction that will be obeyed for up to one hour. However, the number of instructions and the time the entity is compelled to stay in the real world may both be extended by a character of sufficient power.

For each additional instruction issued *or* each additional hour the entity is required to remain in the real world, another Control check must be made with a cumulative – 2 penalty. If any of these additional Control checks are failed, the entity will become uncontrolled with the consequences described below. No more instructions or additional hours may be added to the entity's service as it is now free to exact its vengeance.

Note that any of these additional instructions or extended hours *must* be attempted straight after the first Control check. They may not be added to the entity's service at a later time, so a psyker must plan in advance to decide exactly what he will ask the creature to do if the summoning proves successful.

Failure

It happens to every psyker sooner or later. Despite painstaking attention to detail during the summoning the psyker will, at some point, lose control of the entity he is calling. Even those careful not to overreach themselves may make a mistake – the fact that it is far easier to summon than control makes this almost inevitable.

There are many terrible fates to which a practitioner may be subjected to by an uncontrolled entity. The reactions of most entities are always predictable and deadly - their first priority is the destruction of the mortal who called them into the real world. The failure of the Control check negates the bonds placed on the entity by the summoning and the character's mind, allowing it to act with complete freedom of will. It will move with all speed to the psyker and attack with every resource it has. Once the psyker is slain, it will either seek out and destroy all intelligent life for a period of one hour or simply return to its home dimension, as determined by the Games Master. It will also immediately return to its own dimension if it is in danger of being slain.

In Summary

This concludes the basic rules for summoning and controlling psychic entities. The fledgling psyker will be able to summon all manner of creatures from the infernal planes, provided he does his research. The likes of

---

Summoning in Practice

Phoebe Katz is a 7th level Citizen (rogue psyker) attempting to summon her very first entity. Having calmed her mind with suitable meditations, she feels reasonably confident that she can now summon a ghoul, one of the weaker entities existing in other dimensions.

Being her first attempt in the art, Phoebe makes sure she will be undisturbed during the summoning and takes her time, gaining the +2 Slow Ritual bonus to both her Summoning and Control checks.

Taking eight hours (double that normally required) to perform the summoning, as she is making sure no mistakes enter her preparations, Phoebe attempts to call a ghoul from another dimension. A ghoul has 4 Hit Dice, so the check becomes DC 14. However, Phoebe is a 7th level character (+7), has an Intelligence of 13 (+1), and is taking her time (+2), giving a total bonus of +10, meaning only a 4 needs to be rolled. Unsurprisingly, she manages to call the ghoul to the real world.

Now comes the tricky bit. Incensed at being pulled from its home dimension, the ghoul would clearly like to exact revenge upon Phoebe. Clearing her mind of the threats the ghoul is hurling at her, Phoebe attempts to control the entity.

The Control check is DC 18 as the ghoul's Hit Dice is doubled for this check. Phoebe's Charisma of 11 adds no bonus, but being a 7th level character helps (+1), as does her Slow Ritual (+2), meaning she has to roll 15 or more. With a breath of relief, she succeeds and gives the ghoul a very simple instruction – 'protect me from all harm.' The ghoul will now effectively act as her bodyguard for the next hour but Phoebe, overjoyed at her success, wants more. She exerts her will to force the ghoul to follow this instruction for another hour. There is a –2 penalty to this next Control check as it counts as being an additional instruction, so Phoebe needs to roll a 17.

She succeeds in this too and decides she can try for a third hour. The cumulative penalty for another additional instruction rises to –4, thus requiring a roll of 19 this time around. This time Phoebe fails and the ghoul breaks free of the psychic bonds Phoebe has placed around it. She is about to learn even a ghoul can be a very dangerous enemy when free...

ghouls, ghosts and minor demons will all be within his power to command.

There is, of course, far more to the practice of summoning psychic entities than this. Far more powerful creatures can be called upon as the psyker becomes increasingly more capable and he will be able to command them to do far more things once summoned. He may even be able to draw upon their raw psychic power to fuel his own manifestations to greater levels than he ever dreamed.

Advanced Summonings

Up to now, we have looked at how those skilled in dimensionalist powers can summon creatures from other dimensions. What follows now is a look at more advanced practices and tricks that can be employed during any summoning. The accomplished psyker will now be able to use an entity's raw energy to fuel his own psychic capabilities or to possess other sentient beings. The secrets of group summonings and blood sacrifices are also covered to grant a psyker a further edge in the art. The dangers in dealing with the more advanced forms of summoning are also higher, however, and we therefore take a look at these too.

Siphon Psychic Energy

Many psykers regularly summon psychic entities for the sole purpose of drawing upon their energies to fuel their own mental powers. Such psychically charged energy can be intoxicating to the senses as it flows through the mind, stimulating awareness and granting the ability to control far greater amounts of psychic power than ordinarily possible.

Siphoning Psychic Energy
To siphon energy from a summoned entity, a psyker must make a successful Control check as normal. Instead of giving it an instruction, however, he may instead draw upon its raw energy. The psyker will gain extra power points, based on the Hit Dice of the entity. Each Hit Dice will grant ten bonus power points. These power points may take the character above his normal maximum though they will disappear if not used after a period of 2d6 hours.

A ghoul (4 Hit Dice), for example, could be used to obtain 40 bonus power points.

The entity returns to its home dimension as soon as the energy has been taken from it.

Multiple Summonings

Though it is essential that a psyker does not push himself too far too fast when attempting a summoning, there are many who succumb to temptation. Skilled and powerful characters may attempt to summon more than one psychic entity at a time. This has the advantage of him being able to control two or more entities simultaneously but is, naturally, far more difficult to accomplish. The psyker runs the very real risk of having to face several entities at once if he fails to control them.

Attempting a Multiple Summonation
There is no limit to the total number of entities that may be summoned at any one time and they need not be of the same type. The Hit Dice of all entities to be summoned are totalled for both the Summoning and Control checks. Any instructions given will be applied equally to all the entities – separate instructions cannot be given for each.

There is an additional and cumulative –1 penalty to the Control check for every entity, including the first, summoned.

This special ability potentially provides a very easy route for a psyker to overreach himself when summoning, and that is all we will say on the matter!

Blood Sacrifices

The archetypal dimensionalist, for many ignorant citizens, is one who performs the most hideous ritual sacrifices in the pursuit of his black art. The truth is a little different and many psykers actually shun such practices. Others limit themselves to using only common creatures, such as mutated vermin and other undesirable animals.

It is an undeniable fact though that entities of all type delight in both the misery and death of other creatures. A blood sacrifice may be incorporated into any summoning ritual by a psyker and, in doing so, be granted a little extra leverage in compelling the entity to service.

Using Blood Sacrifices
Any warm-blooded creature, from a chicken to a judge, may be used as a blood sacrifice in a summoning. The creature must be alive, though not necessarily aware,

throughout the summoning and must be slain by the psyker immediately before the entity is drawn into the real world at its completion.

A blood sacrifice adds a +1 bonus to the Control check for any type of entity.

Soul Sacrifices

The single greatest advantage a psyker can have over any being of another dimension in the normal course of summoning is a soul to offer. It is this practice alone that is responsible for so many dark stories and rumours that revolve around demons and their followers. In offering the soul of another sentient being to an entity in return for service, the psyker is doing far more than merely slaying his victim. He is condemning the immortal soul to an eternity of pain, torture and anguish as the plaything and pawn of the entity. This repugnant practice is believed necessary by many of the more skilled psykers, for a suitable sacrifice may convince even the greatest entities to comply to instruction, such is the boon they receive upon returning to their dimension.

The actual process of performing a soul sacrifice is relatively simple and any psyker can readily adapt a summoning to incorporate the extra power to be gained by this practice. The main requirement is a living human or sentient alien – no beast or animal will be sufficient, for these only fulfil the requirements of a blood sacrifice. The victim must be alive and aware throughout the long summoning ritual. At the completion of the summoning, just as the entity is about to appear and be made manifest, the psyker slays his victim, usually by the application of a knife through the heart. At this point, the victim's soul departs, to be immediately snatched by the arriving entity and is lost for eternity, whether or not the psyker succeeds in controlling the entity.

The psyker is likely to gain an immense advantage over the entity as he seeks to control it but the soul of the victim must suffer in return. Forever will the soul wander other dimensions, wreathed in flame and tormented by fell creatures as it is used in the eternal wars of other worlds.

Using Soul Sacrifices

The victim must be kept alive, aware and immobile throughout the ritual. So long as this is accomplished, the slaying of the victim may be considered automatic, regardless of hit point considerations. The slaying of the victim takes place after the Summoning check, but before the Control check.

If the victim escapes or is rescued during the ritual, then the Summoning check automatically fails and all power points are wasted as normal. If the Summoning check is successful but the victim is able to gain freedom just as the psyker prepares to make the sacrifice, the entity appears and the Control check automatically fails with the usual consequences.

A successful soul sacrifice, however, is likely to grant the psyker a tremendous bonus to his Control check. This bonus is equal to the character level or Hit Dice of the victim, whichever is higher.

A soul sacrifice may never be combined with a blood sacrifice and only one victim may be used in a summoning.

Group Summonings

It is a very rare occurrence, but psykers have been known to combine their powers in order to perform a particularly difficult summoning. Such gatherings are often fraught with mistrust, even treachery, but it is often the only way a psyker can summon the more powerful entities of other dimensions with any degree of safety.

Performing a Group Summoning
Any summoning may be developed into a group summoning by a psyker. Only other psykers are permitted to take part. One psyker must lead the summoning and it is upon his skill and ability the attempt is based. The others, however, will add a bonus to both the Summoning and Control checks according to their character level.

Total the character levels of each psyker present and divide this by three, rounding down. The result is the bonus used for the Summoning and Control checks. A maximum of six characters may take part in a group summoning.

Dismissing Entities

There may come a time when a psyker is required to end the service of an entity prematurely. Such circumstances can be many and varied, coming to peace with an enemy the entity has been summoned to fight being one such example.

In these cases, a psyker is required to make a Dismiss check (1d20 + the psyker's Charisma modifier) during the entity's service. This Dismiss check is at DC 10 + the

entity's Hit Dice and may only be attempted against an entity the psyker himself summoned. He must be within 30 feet of the entity and it must not be in total cover relative to him. One attempt may be made to dismiss the entity every round and this is counted as a full-round action. Success in this Dismiss check will result in the entity immediately returning to its home dimension.

As must be abundantly clear, a psyker must instruct his entities carefully, particularly if they are powerful beings in their own right. An entity poorly instructed and unleashed upon the world can cause an immense amount of damage with the psyker being almost powerless to stop it.

Possession

The more powerful entities have the ability to possess mortal beings, subjugating the host to their complete domination. This is usually done either to cause the maximum amount of harm to the mortal who dared to summon them or to stay within the real world for protracted periods of time in order to fulfil their own malevolent plans outside of other dimensions. Accomplished psykers can also force the possession of other mortals as a means to trap the entity in the real world for longer than the summoning might ordinarily allow.

The subject of possession will lose all control of his body, though he remains conscious and aware. The entity takes control of his body utterly and the victim can do nothing more than watch mutely as the entity performs the most vile and hideous of acts in his name. Physical changes also take place, with the body straining to take the shape of both mortal and entity simultaneously. With some entities, the physical effects may be lessened – a succubus possessing a female citizen, for example, may result in nothing more than the softening of features and the growing of vestigial wings. A human body straining to contain a powerful demon though is likely to cause a twisting beyond all recognition. Bones will grow and reshape, muscles will swell and skin change and reform into the likeness of the entity.

For the victim, this is a process almost beyond all endurance, for being aware and a witness to these terrible transformations, they must suffer the absolute agony of the reformation of their bodies. Many go mad during these short seconds alone, others as they are forced to occupy the same mental space as the ultimate evil of a psychic entity. The physical and mental effects possession causes are permanent with no real cure. Even if the entity can be driven out of a host, the victim is likely to be left crippled and unable to function within normal society. Such is the price for succumbing to the entity.

Accidental Possession

Only entities of at least 10 Hit Dice can attempt to possess a mortal being by their own power. If the Control check is failed during a summoning, a Games Master may rule that instead of attacking the psyker, the entity will attempt possession. This is a full round action for the entity.

The character must make a successful Will Save at DC 10 + the entity's Hit Dice to resist the possession attempt. If the summoner passes the Will Save, the entity may never attempt to possess him again. If the Will Save is failed, the entity's attempt at possession is successful and the character is in very serious trouble indeed.

The psyker will immediately come under the complete domination of the entity and effectively becomes an non-player character under the control of the Games Master (though those interested in role-playing may relish the idea of trying their hand at a diabolical character, for however short a period of time).

Physically, a number of things now happen. First, all ability scores and Hit Points are averaged between host and entity into new scores, rounding down. The host will gain all special abilities, skills and saving throw bonuses of the possessing entity. Finally, a melding of the physical forms of host and entity will occur – the Games Master will inform the player concerned of the specific details. As an incidental consequence, the host also gains the immortality of the entity, their body now driven and sustained by raw psychic energy.

At the discretion of the Games Master, the host body may also gain one or more of the physical attacks of the possessing entity, with claw and bite attacks being the most common.

These effects will remain until the entity leaves the host body, though physical changes to appearance are permanent. An entity may choose to leave the host body at any time to return to its home dimension, though as entities are immortal creatures who have existed for aeons, this may well not occur for a great many years,

decades or centuries. The host may, however, be able to exert the innate willpower to drive the entity out. This is entirely dependant on the foothold the entity managed to gain during the act of possession which is determined by the amount the victim failed the Will Save, as detailed on the Possession Table below. Even after regaining control, the victim is likely to be seriously damaged in both mind and body. The side effects on the Possession Table below are applied immediately after the entity leaves the host body and the effects are, again, permanent. Where ability scores must be modified, the player concerned may choose which are affected and reductions may be spread across several ability scores if desired. In addition, the victim will also be reduced to one hit point as his body is wracked with the strain of having contained the entity for however short a period of time.

The *psychic surgery* power is the only way to mitigate the side effects of possession, though it will not be able to cure any physical changes. From this point on, the character will be, at best, considered a mutant and at worst an aberration Psi-Division will be all too keen to get their hands upon to conduct a variety of soul-destroying experiments.

If a period of possession falls in-between any of the limits listed below, as can happen with self-possession, for instance, then the next highest side-effect is used. A character possessed for 3 hours, for example, will suffer the effects of having been possessed for a day.

Possession Table

Will Save failed by	Time Possessed	Side Effects
1-3	1 hour	-1 Wis and Cha, -1,000 XP
4-8	1 day	-1d6 ability scores, -1,000 XP
8-12	1 year	-1d6 ability scores, - 1d6 x 1,000 XP
13+	Permanent	-2d6 ability scores, - 2d6 x 1,000 XP

Possessing Others

In order to gain the service of an entity for a greater length of time, a psyker with few morals may attempt the difficult process of forcing the entity into a mortal host. Whilst few entities find the act of possessing distasteful, doing so at the behest of a summoner can leave them under his control for longer periods, something they will strenuously try to avoid. The strength of will of the psyker can permit any type of psychic entity to possess a host, even those of less than 10 Hit Dice, so even a lowly ghoul may be utilised in this way.

To possess another, the psyker must have another sentient being immobile and present throughout the summoning. Further-more, such a victim must be conscious and aware throughout and so a psyker must devise his own methods for holding subjects ready for possession during the lengthy summoning process. The entity can then be summoned as normal.

There is an additional –4 penalty to the Control check when attempting to force an entity to possess another as it is virtual imprisonment for the entity concerned and it will battle that much harder to circumvent the psyker's will.

The psyker must specify his instruction to the entity during the Control check as normal and this is what the entity will be compelled to do for as long as it possesses the victim. If the Control check fails, the character loses all control of the entity and it will attack him immediately (and may attempt to possess him in return!). If the Control check is successful, then the victim must make a Will Save to avoid possession by the entity, as described in the previous Accidental Possession section. The psyker may apply his Charisma modifier as a bonus to the entity's roll as he exerts his own will alongside that of the entity's to break down the mental defences of the victim and force the possession through. If the victim is willing at the point of possession (immediately after the Control check), then no Will Save takes place – the entity possesses the victim permanently, as if the Will Save had been failed by 13 or more.

If the possession fails, the entity will immediately return to its dimension and the whole attempt is a wasted exercise. If it succeeds, possession occurs as described in the Accidental Possession section, with the full effects being applied to the victim. The only exceptions are that the entity may not return to its home dimension until the duration of the possession is over and that neither it nor the host have free will – both are subject to the instructions given by the psyker before the possession took place.

Exorcism

It is entirely possible that friends of a victim of possession will seek every means to drive out the entity and allow their companion to return to something approaching normality. Powerful psykers may attempt to drive the entity out by sheer force of will, though this never leaves the victim unharmed and completely whole.

Any psi-talented character may attempt to drive an entity out of a victim The entity will seek to avoid the attempt at all costs, fleeing if it is able or actively attacking the psyker. The psyker may either use the *exorcise* power, or his sheer mental energy, as described below.

In order to drive out the entity, the character must make an Exorcism check, rolling 1d20 + his Charisma modifier. If this check equals or exceeds the entity's Hit Dice, he may proceed with the exorcism as he gains measure of the foe he must mentally battle with. If the Exorcism check rolls less than the entity's Hit Dice, then the psyker may never again attempt to drive out the entity – it is simply too powerful and wily for the psyker to force out.

If the Exorcism check proves successful, the psyker immediately rolls 1d6 + his character level + his Charisma modifier. If this beats the entity's Hit Dice, it has been completely forced out of the host body and will materialise in its true form, seeking to attack the psyker that drove it out. It will remain in the real world for a period of one hour, during which time it will likely try to hunt down the psyker who originally forced its possession, or will simply seek to cause as much destruction to mortal life as it is able. The victim will suffer the side-effects for possession as normal.

An attempt to drive out an entity may only be attempted once every 24 hours and is considered to be a full round action. The psyker attempting the task must remain within 5 feet of the victim throughout the process.

Self-Possession

There are more than a few psykers who, upon witnessing the effects of possession on others, are driven to uncover the forbidden knowledge of taking the entity into themselves in an effort to harness its power through more direct means. Only a tiny fraction of these individuals will go through the black rites required, for the dangers are all too apparent. By allowing an entity to enter both mind and body, the psyker is confronting the greatest of evils within the most personal of battlefields. The creature is by no means a passive observer and constantly twists and turns inside his darkest mental recesses, trying to assert its own control as it continually plagues him with the most horrific of nightmare visions and dreams.

Outwardly, the psyker suffers all the torture and damage any other victim of possession does, as his body reshapes itself agonisingly to adopt the form of both man and entity. However, he also gains the entity's strength, power and knowledge, and it is these boons the psyker seeks to the detriment of all else. A psyker skilled in self-possession truly knows the ecstasy of being far more than a mere mortal. So long as he can keep the entity at bay through sheer force of will, he will be the equal of almost anything he sets his imagination to. In doing so, though, the character suffers permanent disfigurement and runs the risk of the entity overpowering his mental strength.

Exchanging the practice of summoning to become one of the possessed, such characters slowly bargain away their souls by fractions through intimate and insidious pacts with infernal creatures of other worlds. Down this route lies possibly the greatest power known but journey's end can only ever be damnation.

Performing Self-Possession

A practitioner must have a manifester level of 12 or more before he may attempt any self-possession. In addition, this is something only specialised dimensionalists may attempt. Any entity successfully summoned and controlled may be compelled to possess the psyker himself in lieu of any other instructions. The character must specify the length of time the self-possession is to last, up to a period of one year and a day. He immediately suffers all the bonuses and penalties for possession as described above, with one exception – he retains free will and is not subject to the wishes of the entity. His physical appearance will permanently change, his ability and hit point scores averaged and he will receive all skills, saving throw bonuses and special qualities of the entity. However, he may still act as he pleases and does not become a non-player character.

The entity will constantly strive to gain dominance of the psyker's body though and this battle will rage until the self-possession ends. Every 24 hours after the self-possession begins, the psyker must make a successful Will check at a DC equal to the entity's Hit Dice as it nurtures and marshals its strength to assert its power over

his body. Success will mean the psyker has brought his mental forces to bear and defeats the entity's attempt. Failure will result in the entity flooding, unchecked, through his mind as it gains the upper hand. From this point, the psyker is treated as having been accidentally possessed and so becomes a non-player character. Furthermore, this will be considered a permanent possession as the psyker allowed the entity to enter his body willingly. . .

The self-possession ends automatically when the length of time specified by the psyker is complete. The entity may also be forced out by exorcism, as described above. The psyker may also willingly drive the entity out earlier at any point, simply by making a Will check at a DC 10 + the entity's Hit Dice. This may be attempted only once a day. Failure will result in the entity immediately striking back, trying to take over the psyker's body once more. Make a Will check at a DC equal to the entity's Hit Dice to avoid the possession attempt, as described above.

Possession in Action

Phoebe has progressed quite far in the field of dimensionalism since we last left her. She has now achieved 12th level as a Citizen (rogue psyker) and feels ready to summon a succubus known as the Debaucheress, having learnt of the creature from the notes of another dimensionalist in a rival street gang.

Everything seems to be going fine in the summoning for Phoebe, as always, is taking her time and generally doing everything she can to make sure nothing goes wrong. She easily summons the succubus but as it appears in front if her, the unthinkable happens – Phoebe's player rolls a 1 for the Control check. Grinning with the lovely maliciousness only a succubus can master, the Debaucheress advances forward towards Phoebe. Fearing for her life, Phoebe begins to manifest an offensive power until she realises that the entity is not attacking her directly – it is assaulting her very mind.

Phoebe's Wisdom of 12 will help here as her Will saving throw bonus is now +5. The DC of the save is 10 + the succubus' CR 9. It is a tough roll, needing 14 or more and, rolling 11, Phoebe quickly succumbs to the Debaucheress' mental attack though it will only be able to control her for one hour. She is now possessed and falls under the control of the Games Master until one hour has passed and the succubus returns to its home dimension.

Phoebe, as the host for the succubus, immediately gains all its skills and saving throw bonuses, as well as all its special abilities, such as energy drain, alternate form and tongues. In addition, their ability scores must be averaged out between them. Phoebe's scores are Str 8, Dex 13, Con 9, Int 15, Wis 12, Cha 11. The succubus' scores are Str 13, Dex 13, Con 13, Int 16, Wis 14, Cha 20. The new scores for Phoebe, averaged between her original abilities and those of the succubus are therefore Str 10, Dex 13, Con 11, Int 15, Wis 13, Cha 15. Her hit points of 12 are also averaged with those of the succubus' of 33 to result in 22 hit points.

Last of all, much to Phoebe's consternation, she becomes physically more like the succubus! She starts to grow small bat-like wings and her eyes begin to glow with a sinister light.

Fortunately for Phoebe, the possession lasts only an hour and the succubus soon departs, though not without destroying her hideout in which it was summoned. She loses the succubus' skills and special abilities, and her ability scores and hit points are returned to what they were before the possession took place. She now has, however, full control of her own body again.

The effect, brief as it was, has unfortunately not left Phoebe completely untouched for she still retains the physical likeness of a succubus. She also loses one point from her Wisdom and Charisma ability scores permanently, as well as 1,000 experience points.

The whole affair has left Phoebe questioning whether she will continue the practice of summoning at all – at the very least she is likely to be very cautious in the art for the future. She also realises, however, that the possession could have been much, much worse. Overall, she has got off lightly.

Lords of the Flux

This chapter takes a look at the kind of characters that possess psi-talent and are capable of using it to either fight evil or plan their own villainous crimes. Here you will find new prestige classes, including the renowned exorcist judge, that will allow characters to take full advantage of the rules presented in *The Rookie's Guide to Psi-Talent*, as well as make them a force to be reckoned with in day-to-day life on the streets. Whether you are seeking to banish psychic entities from the real world or make your fortune as a celebrity psi, there is a prestige class for everyone.

The Exorcist Judge

To say that Mega-City One suffers many incursions of psychic entities into the real world would be a falsehood but, due to their supernatural abilities, the presence of a single one can cause immense destruction to both citizens and their property. The Justice Department's Psi-Division set up the Exorcist Squad to deal with just such eventualities – a specialised group of highly skilled psi operatives possessing the strength of will to do battle with the greatest psychic entities and trained in ways to defeat them. Exorcist judges are also called in to deal with the few cases of demonic possession the Psi-Division must handle every year. As individuals, exorcist judges tend to be fiercely dedicated to protecting the city and citizens they serve, risking their lives time and again to face the most powerful creatures to threaten Mega-City One.

Hit Die: d8.

Requirements

To qualify to become an exorcist judge, a psi-judge must fulfil all the following criteria.

Manifester Level: 10th.
Skills: Knowledge (psi-talent) 12 ranks, Knowledge (psychic entities) 4 ranks.
Feats: Enhanced Power, Great Fortitude, Inner Strength, Iron Will, Nerves of Steel.

Class Skills

The exorcist judge's class skills (and the key ability for each skill) are Balance (Dex), Bluff (Cha), Climb (Str), Computer Use (Int), Concentration (Con), Intimidate (Cha), Jump (Str), Knowledge (law) (Int), Knowledge (psi-talent) (Int), Knowledge (psychic entities) (Int), Listen (Wis), Medical (Wis), Psi-Scan (Int), Ride (Dex), Search (Int), Sense Motive (Wis), Spot (Wis), Streetwise (Wis), Swim (Str), and Technical (Int).

Skill points at each level: 2 + Int modifier.

Class Features

All of the following are class features of the exorcist judge prestige class.

Specialist Equipment: In addition to a new uniform, exorcist judges are also granted a psi-focus +1, silver-tipped shells for their Lawgiver and a silver boot knife to supplement their standard issue equipment. The silver-tipped shells replace any one specialist type of ammunition of the judge's choice (such as high explosive, for example). Full details on psi-foci and silver weapons can be found in

PSI DIVISION! I WANT THE **EXORCISTS** DOWN HERE — PRONTO!

The Exorcist Judge

Level	Base Attack Bonus	Fort Save	Ref Save	Will Save	Special
1	+0	+2	+2	+2	Detect Psychic Entity
2	+1	+3	+3	+3	Power Resistance
3	+2	+3	+3	+3	Improved Exorcism
4	+3	+4	+4	+4	Bonus Feat
5	+3	+4	+4	+4	View Paraform
6	+4	+5	+5	+5	Dismiss
7	+5	+5	+5	+5	Magnify Psi-Focus
8	+6/+1	+6	+6	+6	Bonus Feat
9	+6/+1	+6	+6	+6	Smash Psychic Defence
10	+7/+2	+7	+7	+7	Greater Exorcism

Chapter 7. Exorcist judges are forbidden from ever using the *summon psychic entity* power.

Psi-Talent: At every level gained in the exorcist judge prestige class, the character gains new powers and power points as if he had also gained a level in a psi-talented class (such as psi-judge) he belonged to before adding the prestige class. He does not, however, gain any other benefit a character of the original class would have gained (such as bonus feats or hit points beyond those gained with the prestige class), except for the effective increased level of psi-talent.

Detect Psychic Entity: Exorcist judges become attuned to the presence of psychic entities very early on in their training, an ability that can often save their lives in the field as it means that few entities can launch a surprise assault upon one who is properly prepared. The exorcist judge may manifest the *detect psychic entity* power for free, any number of times per day.

Power Resistance: An important part of the exorcist judge's training is being able to resist the psychic powers of the entities he must face in the field. By building up his psychic defences through a series of incredibly harsh and mind-shattering tests, the exorcist judge can tune his mind to the ways psychic entities commonly assault mortals. The character gains a Power Resistance equal to his character level, though this applies to powers manifested by psychic entities only, not other psi-talented characters.

Improved Exorcism: From 3rd level onwards, the exorcist judge's force of will is more than a match for any minor entity that possesses an innocent citizen. He may add his class level to any Exorcism check (see p52) he is required to make.

Bonus Feat: Exorcist judges are some of the best trained and most valued operatives within Psi-Division. At 4th and 8th level, the exorcist judge receives a bonus Judge, Metapsi or Psi feat of his choice, in addition to feats normally gained every three character levels.

View Paraform: Upon reaching 5th level, the exorcist judge is highly skilled at hunting down psychic entities, even when they try to avoid his search. By casting his mind forward into the barriers between dimensions, the exorcist judge is capable of detecting even entities that are normally invisible. He treats any invisible psychic entity within 10 feet as being visible.

Dismiss: Exorcist judges are trained well in hurling psychic entities back to their home dimensions with the force of their mind alone. The exorcist judge may manifest the *dismiss* power for free, any number of times per day.

Magnify Psi-Focus: On reaching 7th level, exorcist judges learn how to take the best advantage of any psi-focus they possess or come into contact with. The exorcist judge doubles the benefit of any psi-focus he uses. For example, a psi-focus +1 will now be treated as a psi-focus +2.

Smash Psychic Defence: The greatest psychic entities have some of the most formidable psychic defences ever encountered and can render even the greatest psyker almost helpless as manifested powers simply bounce off them. At 9th level, the exorcist judge has become adept at smashing through any psychic defence with just a simple thought. He may add his class level to any Manifester check he makes to break through Power Resistance.

Greater Exorcism: At 10th level, the exorcist judge reaches the pinnacle of his capabilities and few possessing psychic entities are able to resist his raw force of will. The exorcist judge automatically succeeds in any Exorcist check he is called to make and if he is able to force the entity out of the host body, it will not materialise in the real world, but will instantly be sent back to its home dimension.

The Celebrity Psi

Rogue psykers are ruthlessly hunted down by Psi-Division, for the good of all citizens in Mega-City One. One untrained and undisciplined psyker can use his psi-talent for any number of criminal ends or, worse, become a conduit for psychic entities seeking to gain entry to the real world. Most psi-talented citizens who wish to avoid incarceration in the psi-cubes are therefore driven underground, where they pawn their services to vicious street gangs and criminal organisations. A few, however, are drawn by the glamour and credits offered by the more successful pirate vid-stations, who delight in being able to offer their audiences genuine psychic displays. A psyker doing the pirate vid circuit can become a celebrity of no little renown in a remarkably short time and, while he must spend the rest of his life looking over his shoulder for judges hot on his trail, the credits that keep rolling in can buy a lot of security and safety.

Hit Die: d6.

Requirements

To qualify to become a celebrity psi, a citizen must fulfil all the following criteria.

Manifester Level: 5th.
Known Powers: At least three of the following: *concussion, control body, control flames, enrapture, incinerating finger, levitate, minor telekinesis, pyrokinetic burst, resist flames, sheet of flame, suggestion* or *summon psychic entity.*

Class Skills

The celebrity psi's class skills (and the key ability for each skill) are Bluff (Cha), Concentration (Con), Intimidate (Cha), Knowledge (psi-talent) (Int), Psi-Scan (Int), and Sense Motive (Wis).

Skill points at each level: 4 + Int modifier.

Class Features

All of the following are class features of the celebrity psi prestige class.

Psi-Talent: At every level gained in the celebrity psi prestige class, the character gains new powers and power points as if he had also gained a level in a psi-talented class (such as Citizen – rogue psyker) he belonged to before adding the prestige class. He does not, however, gain any other benefit a character of the original class would have gained (such as bonus feats or hit points beyond those gained with the prestige class), except for the effective increased level of psi-talent.

Celebrity Appearance: The more skilled a celebrity psi becomes at enhancing his shows with flashy effects, the more in demand he becomes and thus the greater he can charge pirate vid-stations for each appearance. The celebrity psi gains 500 credits per class level for each appearance he makes on a pirate vid-station in his capacity as a celebrity. However, he will soon find that the judges are very quick to clamp down on any pirate broadcast, particularly those featuring rogue psykers, and he runs a very real risk of being hunted down and arrested with each appearance, as determined by the Games Master.

Flashy Effects: Flashy effects are the trademark of the celebrity psi and he quickly learns how to use them to overawe non psi-talented characters. Whenever the celebrity psi manifests a power, he may choose to include flashy effects, an array of colours, lights, flashing rays,

The Celebrity Psi

Level	Base Attack Bonus	Fort Save	Ref Save	Will Save	Special
1	+0	+0	+0	+2	Celebrity Appearance
2	+1	+0	+0	+3	Flashy Effects
3	+2	+1	+1	+3	Notoriety
4	+3	+1	+1	+4	Celebrity Specialist
5	+3	+1	+1	+4	Bedazzle

spooky sounds and other spectral displays to accompany the power. Such effects have no real substance and only serve to frighten or awe those with no knowledge of psychic powers. Any non psi-talented character subject to a power enhanced with flashy effects suffers a –2 morale penalty to any saving throw he is called upon to make in order to resist the power. Psi-talented characters know far better, and are not affected by the charlatan.

Notoriety: By the time he reaches 3rd level, the celebrity psi will have achieved no little renown and will likely be in demand by several pirate vid-stations. He may even start becoming a household name across an entire sector as citizens illegally tune in to his broadcasts. He can now demand 1,000 credits per class level for each appearance he makes. However, the celebrity psi is now well known to the Justice Department and if he is ever caught and successfully identified by a judge, no amount of bluffing will be able to avoid him being sent to the psi-cubes for his crimes.

Celebrity Specialist: Though few celebrity psis are true specialists, many do start to become very good at their own trade. From 4th level, the celebrity psi is considered to be a specialist (and so gain the +2 bonus to the DC of their saving throws of manifested powers) whenever using the following powers: *concussion, control body, control flames, domination, enrapture, greater telekinesis, incinerating finger, levitate, mass concussion, mass domination, mass suggestion, minor telekinesis, pyrokinetic burst, telekinesis, resist flames, sheet of flame, suggestion* or *summon psychic entity.*

Bedazzle: At 5th level, the celebrity psi is a true master of his art and can combine greater amounts of flashy effects into his displays. However, his bedazzling effects now have some substance and can have some minor effect even on psi-talented characters. Any non psi-talented character subject to a power enhanced by bedazzle suffers

a –4 morale penalty to any saving throw he is called upon to make in order to resist the power. In addition, the celebrity psi gains a +4 circumstance bonus to any Manifester check he makes in order to defeat any Power Resistance.

The Conduit

Among all the rogue psykers hiding in the dark places of Mega-City One, it is the conduit that Psi-Division perhaps fears the most. Not content to court the supernatural powers of psychic entities brought to the real world by his sheer mental will, the conduit willingly allows such baleful creatures to enter his body in order to tap their raw dimensional energy. The conduit can be a fearsome opponent to face in combat but few survive very long, wracked by the changes their bodies go through every time a new psychic entity is introduced into their mind. While conduits have sufficient mental and physical strength to nullify the side-effects of possession, even they will eventually succumb to the changes forced upon them as more and more psychic entities are allowed to travel through their minds.

Hit Die: d8.

Requirements
To qualify to become a conduit, a citizen must fulfil all the following criteria.

Manifester Level: 12th.
Specialist: Dimensionalist.
Known Powers: *Summon psychic entity.*
Constitution: 15+.
Skills: Knowledge (psi-talent) 8 ranks, Knowledge (psychic entities) 15 ranks.
Feats: Great Fortitude, Permanent Control, Specialist Focus (dimensionalist), Strength of Will.

The Conduit

Level	Base Attack Bonus	Fort Save	Ref Save	Will Save	Special
1	+0	+2	+0	+0	Dimensional Link
2	+1	+3	+0	+0	Entity Traits (2)
3	+2	+3	+1	+1	Entity Traits (3)
4	+3	+4	+1	+1	Entity Traits (4)
5	+3	+4	+1	+1	Entity Traits (5)

Class Skills

The conduit's class skills (and the key ability for each skill) are Bluff (Cha), Concentration (Con), Intimidate (Cha), Knowledge (psi-talent) (Int), Knowledge (psychic entities) (Int), and Sense Motive (Wis).

Skill points at each level: 4 + Int modifier.

Class Features

All of the following are class features of the conduit prestige class.

Psi-Talent: At every level gained in the conduit prestige class, the character gains new powers and power points as if he had also gained a level in a psi-talented class (such as Citizen – rogue psyker) he belonged to before adding the prestige class. He does not, however, gain any other benefit a character of the original class would have gained (such as bonus feats or hit points beyond those gained with the prestige class), except for the effective increased level of psi-talent.

Dimensional Link: The conduit has the remarkable ability to forge permanent links between himself and powerful psychic entities of other dimensions. He can automatically do this with any psychic entity he successfully summons and controls (see Chapter 5 for full details). As soon as this link is forged, the conduit automatically loses 1d6 points permanently from his Strength, Dexterity and Constitution ability scores. The conduit may freely choose which ability scores suffer this loss and it may be spread across two or three ability scores as appropriate. If any ability score is reduced to 0 in this way, the conduit is immediately killed by the very powers he sought to harness. This loss cannot be negated

through the use of *psychic surgery*. From this point on, the conduit may call upon any psychic entity he has forged a dimensional link to as a full round action. He will immediately gain any one single trait from the psychic entity he desires – this may be an ability score (such as Strength), its attacks, speed, a skill, feat, special quality or special attack. This effect will last for one hour. Only one psychic entity can be called upon in this way at a time and dimensional link may be used a maximum number of times per day equal to the conduit's class level. However, the conduit can end this possession at any time as a full round action and does not suffer any of the side effects of possession as described on p50. During this time, the conduit will assume many of the outward features of the psychic entity he is sharing his body with, gaining stature, fangs, horns, wings and skin colour as appropriate. When the dimensional link ends, his physique will return to normal, though his appearance will gradually change over a period of months to reflect the psychic entities that regularly share his body, as determined by the Games Master.

Entity Traits: As the conduit rises in level, so too does his ability to harness the power of psychic entities increase. Additional traits may be used every time a psychic entity is called upon, as shown on the table below. For example, a 3rd level conduit can take three traits from any psychic entity he has a dimensional link with – if he were to have such a link with a succubus, he could take her Charisma, wings and ecstatic kiss.

The Faith Healer

Faith healers are a relatively common variation of rogue psyker, though many are unaware of the psychic talent they possess and merely assume their healing hands are

The Faith Healer

Level	Base Attack Bonus	Fort Save	Ref Save	Will Save	Special
1	+0	+0	+0	+2	Healing Hands
2	+1	+0	+0	+3	Cure Disease
3	+2	+1	+1	+3	Cure Poison
4	+3	+1	+1	+4	Cure Radiation
5	+3	+1	+1	+4	Raise the Dead

either a natural ability or are Grud-given. They are also amongst the least dangerous and threatening of rogues, though Psi-Division is still keen to track them down for their unique talents and abilities. A good faith healer can cure almost any injury or disease simply by touching the afflicted and so has obvious benefits to any street gang or criminal organisation that wishes to avoid its members travelling to public med centres. They are also often found at the heart of secret cults, where a faith healer possessing any kind of leadership quality will find it easy to convince weaker minded citizens that they are truly blessed by Grud. The very best faith healers are able to combine their ability to heal any injury with a superb medical knowledge, but all too many rely solely on their own natural abilities.

Hit Die: d6.

Requirements
To qualify to become a faith healer, a citizen must fulfil all the following criteria.

Manifester Level: 3rd.
Known Powers: *Empathic transfer.*

Class Skills
The faith healer's class skills (and the key ability for each skill) are Concentration (Con), Knowledge (psi-talent) (Int), Medical (Wis), Sense Motive (Wis), and Technical (Int).

Skill points at each level: 6 + Int modifier.

Class Features
All of the following are class features of the faith healer prestige class.

Psi-Talent: At every level gained in the faith healer prestige class, the character gains new powers and power points as if he had also gained a level in a psi-talented class (such as Citizen – rogue psyker) he belonged to

before adding the prestige class. He does not, however, gain any other benefit a character of the original class would have gained (such as bonus feats or hit points beyond those gained with the prestige class), except for the effective increased level of psi-talent.

Healing Hands: The primary ability of any faith healer is to heal physical injuries simply by touching the afflicted. As a full round action, the faith healer can use his healing hands upon any living creature. The creature will be healed an amount of hit points equal to the amount of power points the faith healer chooses to expend.

Cure Disease: Even the most hideous of diseases can be cured by a competent faith healer. At 2nd level, simply by touching a living creature afflicted by disease, the faith healer can attempt to remove any one disease as a full round action. The faith healer must make a Will save at a DC equal to the Fortitude DC of the disease itself. If successful, the disease is immediately removed from the victim. Using cure disease requires the expenditure of 10 power points. This will not cure any effects suffered from the disease, merely remove the disease itself.

Cure Poison: Poisons are much more difficult to treat than diseases, as they can quickly flood an entire system and their effects are usually swift. A faith healer can cure any living creature suffering the effects of poison by touch, as a full round action. This requires the expenditure of 15 power points and requires the faith healer succeeds at a Will save at a DC equal to the contact, ingestion, inhalation, or injury DC of the poison itself. This will not cure any effects already suffered from the poison, merely remove the poison itself.

Cure Radiation: At 4th level, the faith healer has sufficient ability to cure even Radiation sickness, an incredible feat of psychic power. This is performed in the same way as for cure disease, except that 20 power points are expended with each attempt and the Will save required by the faith healer is made at a DC equal to the Fortitude DC of the radiation source.

Raise the Dead: Perhaps the most staggering ability of any faith healer is to be able to literally awaken the dead and bring a corpse back to life. Very few faith healers ever reach this level of ability and most are subsequently forced into seclusion as their abilities are sought after by many anxious citizens. A faith healer can bring back to life any living creature that has died from hit point loss, disease, poison or radiation simply by touching them, as a full round action. However, the faith healer must attempt this within one round of the creature actually dying, or the attempt will automatically fail. This requires the expenditure of 30 power points.

The Psychic Master

It is only within the harsh training environment of Psi-Division that psykers can truly fulfil the real potential of their psi-talent. Rogue psykers lack the discipline and training of psi-judges and so will always be at a disadvantage on the streets unless they have the backing of powerful perps. A tiny fraction of rogue psykers, however, do find the capability to vastly extend their powers. Whether it is through a seminal and demanding event in their lives, or merely through extended contemplation and meditation, these psychic masters are capable of accessing tremendous mental energies. With dedication and strong will, a psychic master can rival or even surpass the best operatives Psi-Division has to offer.

Hit Die: d4.

Requirements
To qualify to become a psychic master, a citizen must fulfil all the following criteria.

Manifester Level: 10th.
Skills: Knowledge (psi-talent) 12 ranks, Psi-Scan 12 ranks.
Feats: Encompassing Power, Enhanced Power, Magnify Power, Quicken Power.

Special: Must train for three consecutive months in solitude, or for one month under the supervision of a 5th level psychic master.

Class Skills
The psychic master's class skills (and the key ability for each skill) are Balance (Dex), Climb (Str), Concentration (Con), Intimidate (Cha), Jump (Str), Knowledge (psi-talent) (Int), Listen (Wis), Psi-Scan (Int), Search (Int), Sense Motive (Wis), Spot (Wis), and Swim (Str).

Skill points at each level: 4 + Int modifier.

Class Features
All of the following are class features of the psychic master prestige class.

Psi-Talent: At every level gained in the psychic master prestige class, the character gains new powers and power points as if he had also gained a level in a psi-talented class (such as Citizen – rogue psyker) he belonged to before adding the prestige class. He does not, however, gain any other benefit a character of the original class would have gained (such as bonus feats or hit points beyond those gained with the prestige class), except for the effective increased level of psi-talent.

Psychic Mastery: The psychic master has access to a level of psi-talent only dreamed of by most rogue psykers on the streets. Upon gaining the psychic master prestige class, the character from now on uses the psi-judge Powers Known table on page 15 of the *Judge Dredd Rulebook*, or on p12 of this book if he is a specialist. He will immediately gain new powers as indicated by these tables. From this point on, the psychic master uses this table to calculate which powers he gains as he increases in level.

Bonus Power Points: The psychic master has incredible mental reserves and can often outlast even more powerful psykers in a sustained psychic duel. At 2nd and 4th level, the psychic master gains a number of extra power points as indicated on the table below, to be added to his total power points per day.

The Psychic Master

Level	Base Attack Bonus	Fort Save	Ref Save	Will Save	Special
1	+0	+0	+0	+2	Psychic Mastery
2	+1	+0	+0	+3	Bonus Power Points (10)
3	+2	+1	+1	+3	Mental Specialisation
4	+3	+1	+1	+4	Bonus Power Points (25)
5	+3	+1	+1	+4	Train Psyker

Mental Specialisation: At 3rd level, the psychic master has sufficiently trained his mind to focus on another area of psi-talent. If he is not a specialist, he may immediately select one area of psychic specialisation (dimensionalist, pre-cog, pyrokine, telekine or telepath), so long as he meets the entry prerequisite. If he is already a specialist, he may select another area of specialisation that he meets the entry prerequisites to, and be considered a specialist on this field also. However many fields of specialisation the psychic master has, he may only gain one bonus power per level (which may be of either specialisation, if he has two).

Train Psyker: At 5th level, there are few secrets in the realms of psi-talent that the psychic master does not possess and have at his control. He may now train other rogue psykers to become psychic masters themselves, so long as they meet the entry requirements of this prestige class. In doing so, he can drastically shorten their training time and so build up a veritable force of powerful psykers.

The Psi-Warlord

There are few opponents more lethal than an angry psi-warlord. Where most psi-talented characters focus their abilities into achieving greater levels of psychic activity, the psi-warlord hones his mental skills for combat. Utterly ruthless in battle, he combines lightning-fast reflexes and superior skill in arms with a mind dedicated to nothing more than the slaying of enemies. Psi-warlords make for superb assassins, though there are few who can afford their services. In any event, many psi-warlords tend to follow their own code of honour that precludes them from launching an attack on anyone but recognised enemies. Others actively seek and hunt down other psi-warlords in order to prove to themselves and the world that they truly are the best fighters.

Hit Die: d10.

Requirements
To qualify to become a psi-warlord, a citizen must fulfil all the following criteria.

Base Attack Bonus: +9.
Manifester Level: 10th.
Skills: Knowledge (psi-talent) 8 ranks, Psi-Scan 8 ranks.
Feats: Combat Reflexes, Endurance, Lightning Reflexes, Quicken Power, Weapon Focus.

Class Skills
The psi-warlord's class skills (and the key ability for each skill) are Balance (Dex), Bluff (Cha), Climb (Str), Concentration (Con), Hide (Dex), Intimidate (Cha), Jump (Str), Knowledge (psi-talent) (Int), Listen (Wis), Medical (Wis), Move Silently (Dex), Psi-Scan (Int), Ride (Dex), Search (Int), Sense Motive (Wis), Spot (Wis), Swim (Str), and Technical (Int).

Skill points at each level: 2 + Int modifier.

Class Features
All of the following are class features of the psi-warlord prestige class.

Psi-Talent: At every level gained in the psi-warlord prestige class, the character gains new powers and power points as if he had also gained a level in a psi-talented class (such as Citizen – rogue psyker) he belonged to before adding the prestige class. He does not, however, gain any other benefit a character of the original class would have gained (such as bonus feats or hit points beyond those gained with the prestige class), except for the effective increased level of psi-talent.

Bonus Feat: Psi-warlord are amongst the most powerful psykers in the world. At 1st, 3rd and 5th level, the psi-warlord receives a bonus General, Metapsi or Psi feat of his choice, in addition to feats normally gained every three character levels.

Favoured Weapon: The psi-warlord spends much of his time in silent contemplation of psychic attacks and

The Psi-Warlord

Level	Base Attack Bonus	Fort Save	Ref Save	Will Save	Special
1	+1	+2	+0	+2	Bonus Feat, Favoured Weapon
2	+2	+3	+0	+3	Study Enemy, Bonus Power Points (10)
3	+3	+3	+1	+3	Bonus Feat
4	+4	+4	+1	+4	Bonus Power Points (10)
5	+5	+4	+1	+4	Bonus Feat

combat tactics, all revolving around the use of one specific weapon. When he fights, the psi-warlord's weapons become an extension not only of his body, but of his will too. The psi-warlord selects one melee or pistol weapon to be his favoured weapon. Whenever he fights, he may add his class level to all attack and damage rolls made with the weapon. In addition he may also add his class level to the weapon's AP score. However, so in tune with this weapon is he that the psi-warlord will now use any other weapon as if he were non-proficient in it (suffering a –4 penalty to attack rolls), regardless of his actual proficiencies.

Study Enemy: Whether he acts as an assassin or simply searches for the greatest fighters he can find, at 2nd level the psi-warlord becomes adept at studying an enemy over a protracted period of time. For every full hour the psi-warlord can watch an enemy, he gains a +1 bonus to all Hide, Listen, Move Silently, Search and Spot checks he makes against him. The maximum bonus attainable through studying an enemy in this way is +5.

Bonus Power Points: The psi-warlord has incredible mental reserves and can often outlast even more powerful psykers in a sustained psychic duel. At 2nd and 4th level, the psychic master gains a number of extra power points as indicated on the table above, to be added to his total power points per day.

The Snake Head

The snake head is the lowest of the low, a punk who has discovered he has the capability to manifest potent psychic powers and yet uses them for nothing more than preying on others of his own kind. He is a potent ally to any street gang but is utterly selfish to the core and retains few loyalties as he drifts through the underworld of Mega-City One. The snake head desires power over other citizens above all else and delights in using his mental powers to dominate others and render them helpless. He is a bully with very real strength and he knows it. Likely as not, the snake head has never met another psyker and so has never had to face an even fight. He truly is scum. As he goes through life, the snake head will amass a great many enemies through his constant bullying and thievery, and so few survive to truly make anything of themselves.

Hit Die: d8.

Requirements
To qualify to become a snake head, a citizen must fulfil all the following criteria.

Manifester Level: 4th.
Skills: Intimidate 6 ranks, Knowledge (psi-talent) 4

The Snake Head

Level	Base Attack Bonus	Fort Save	Ref Save	Will Save	Special
1	+1	+2	+0	+0	Bully and Thieve
2	+2	+3	+0	+0	Summon Lackeys
3	+3	+3	+1	+1	Man of the Block
4	+4	+4	+1	+1	Sixth Sense
5	+5	+4	+1	+1	Improved Summon Lackeys

ranks, Streetwise 6 ranks.

Feats: Skill Focus (streetwise), Toughness.

Class Skills

The snake head's class skills (and the key ability for each skill) are Bluff (Cha), Climb (Str), Hide (Dex), Intimidate (Cha), Jump (Str), Knowledge (psi-talent) (Int), Listen (Wis), Move Silently (Dex), Psi-Scan (Int), Ride (Dex), Search (Int), Sense Motive (Wis), Spot (Wis), Streetwise (Wis), Swim (Str), and Technical (Int).

Skill points at each level: 4 + Int modifier.

Class Features

All of the following are class features of the snake head prestige class.

Psi-Talent: At every level gained in the snake head prestige class, the character gains new powers and power points as if he had also gained a level in a psi-talented class (such as Citizen – rogue psyker) he belonged to before adding the prestige class. He does not, however, gain any other benefit a character of the original class would have gained (such as bonus feats or hit points beyond those gained with the prestige class), except for the effective increased level of psi-talent.

Bully and Thieve: The snake head is a parasite to others and enjoys bullying and thieving from those who cannot stand up to him either physically or mentally. He may use his Streetwise skill in Profession checks in order to determine how many credits per week he can leech out of the other lowlifes around him.

Summon Lackeys: Given 24 uninterrupted hours, the snake head can round up any sycophantic juves who actually look up to him, and wish to emulate their hero's abilities. He will gain 2d6 1st level juves armed with a variety of cheap melee weapons who will be willing to follow his orders for 1d3 hours. This is identical to the punk prior life's ability and they do not stack.

Man of the Block: At 3rd level, the snake head begins to build a serious reputation in his local block and few are willing to stand up to him or gain his attention. The snake head gains a +2 bonus to all Bluff, Intimidate, Sense Motive and Streetwise checks made while within one mile of his home cityblock.

Sixth Sense: By the time he achieves 4th level, even the snake head begins to realise the number of enemies he is beginning to amass, other punks and criminals who would just love to see him taken down a peg or two, or even killed. The snake head gains the Sixth Sense feat, if he did not already possess it, even if he does not meet the prerequisites.

Improved Summon Lackeys: At 5th level, the snake head's reputation knows no bounds and can call upon many more followers to do as he wishes, even if they serve him purely out of fear. This is identical to the Summon Lackeys class feature, but the snake head will gain 4d10 punks or goons in addition to the usual 2d6 juves. Punks and goons will all be of 1st level and will be armed with a variety of cheap melee and pistol weapons.

The Teledominant

There are few highs in the use of psi-talent greater than the ability to completely take over the actions and thoughts of another citizen, to completely rule their lives and control their personalities. After the ability to pull psychic entities into the real world, this is the power Psi-Division fears the most in rogue psykers, for one who can easily control other citizens is one who can commit almost any crime and achieve any goal with ease. The teledominant is a control freak through and through. Having specialised in accessing the thoughts and emotions of other citizens, he now concentrates on actually controlling them. As he grows in power, the teledominant can often become removed from the rest of humanity, viewing them as nothing more than cattle to be used and controlled whenever his whims require action.

It can take incredible mental strength to stand up to a skilled teledominant.

Hit Die: d6.

Requirements
To qualify to become a teledominant, a citizen must fulfil all the following criteria.

Manifester Level: 9th.
Specialist: Telepathy.
Known Powers: *Enrapture, Suggestion, Domination.*
Skills: Concentration 4 ranks, Knowledge (psi-talent) 12 ranks.
Feats: Greater Specialist Focus (telepathy), Power Penetration.

Class Skills
The teledominant's class skills (and the key ability for each skill) are Bluff (Cha), Intimidate (Cha), Knowledge (psi-talent) (Int), Psi-Scan (Int), Search (Int), Sense Motive (Wis), Spot (Wis), and Streetwise (Wis).

Skill points at each level: 4 + Int modifier.

Class Features
All of the following are class features of the teledominant prestige class.

Psi-Talent: At every level gained in the teledominant prestige class, the character gains new powers and power points as if he had also gained a level in a psi-talented class (such as Citizen – rogue psyker) he belonged to before adding the prestige class. He does not, however, gain any other benefit a character of the original class would have gained (such as bonus feats or hit points beyond those gained with the prestige class), except for the effective increased level of psi-talent.

Dominating Will: The teledominant has a fearsome mental strength and few can hold out against it for long. Any creature making a saving throw against any

The Teledominant

Level	Base Attack Bonus	Fort Save	Ref Save	Will Save	Special
1	+0	+0	+0	+2	Dominating Will
2	+1	+0	+0	+3	Psychic Wiles
3	+1	+1	+1	+3	Enrapture
4	+2	+1	+1	+4	Suggestion
5	+2	+1	+1	+4	Domination

telepathic power manifested by the teledominant suffers a morale penalty equal to the teledominant's class level.

Psychic Wiles: At 2nd level, the teledominant can constantly draw minute amounts of psychic energy and use it to influence anyone he talks to. He gains a +2 circumstance bonus to all Bluff, Intimidate and Sense Motive checks against any creature that does not possess any amount of Power Resistance.

Enrapture: On achieving 3rd level, the teledominant can manifest mind controlling powers almost at a whim. He may manifest *enrapture* without paying any power points a number of times per day equal to his Charisma modifier.

Suggestion: At 4th level, the mere words of a teledominant are often enough to command instant respect and obedience. He may manifest *suggestion* without paying any power points a number of times per day equal to his Charisma modifier.

Domination: By the time he reaches 5th level, the teledominant is the master of his art and he can take over victims almost at will. He may manifest *domination* without paying any power points a number of times per day equal to his Charisma modifier.

The Trans-Dime

The trans-dime is a very rare breed of psychic and often practices his talent in secluded places where he will not be disturbed or discovered. Casting his mind across multiple dimensions at once, the trans-dime is one of the foolish mortals who actually seeks to summon, bargain with and control the most powerful psychic entities he can find. Armed with the power granted by these supernatural creatures, the trans-dime is an invaluable addition to any gang or organisation that is not too fussy about the methods employed to defeat rivals. With a trans-dime on the payroll, a rival gang leader who has been enjoying just a little too much success can be sent

an unstoppable demon straight from the pits of hell to halt his activities – permanently. As with all dark powers, however, there is a price to pay and few trans-dimes live to retirement age for there is always the temptation to draw a little too much power from the other dimensions and summon a creature that is far beyond the control of the trans-dime. If he is lucky, he may only be killed by the enraged creature.

Hit Die: d6.

Requirements
To qualify to become a trans-dime, a citizen must fulfil all the following criteria.

Manifester Level: 8th.
Specialist: Dimensionalist.
Known Powers: *Summon psychic entity.*
Skills: Knowledge (psi-talent) 10 ranks, Knowledge (psychic entities) 10 ranks.
Feats: Specialist Focus (dimensionalist).

Class Skills
The trans-dime's class skills (and the key ability for each skill) are Computer Use (Int), Concentration (Con), Knowledge (psi-talent) (Int), Knowledge (psychic entities) (Int), and Technical (Int).

Skill points at each level: 4 + Int modifier.

Class Features
All of the following are class features of the trans-dime prestige class.

Psi-Talent: At every level gained in the trans-dime prestige class, the character gains new powers and power points as if he had also gained a level in a psi-talented class (such as Citizen – rogue psyker) he belonged to before adding the prestige class. He does not, however, gain any other benefit a character of the original class would have gained (such as bonus feats or hit points

The Trans-Dime

Level	Base Attack Bonus	Fort Save	Ref Save	Will Save	Special
1	+0	+0	+0	+2	Lesser Control
2	+1	+0	+0	+3	Extended Instruction
3	+1	+1	+1	+3	Entity Dominance
4	+2	+1	+1	+4	Full Instruction
5	+2	+1	+1	+4	Improved Control

beyond those gained with the prestige class), except for the effective increased level of psi-talent.

Lesser Control: At 1st level, the trans-dime has the strength of will to compel psychic entities to serve him for longer periods of time. The maximum time a psychic entity can stay in the real world is increased to two hours. Each successive Control check to retain the services of the psychic entity for longer will now allow it to stay a further two hours in the real world instead of just one.

Extended Instruction: At 2nd level, a trans-dime grows strong enough to compel the psychic entities he summons to follow longer and more complicated instructions. The limit for each instruction issued increases to twelve words.

Entity Dominance: As the trans-dime's skill and knowledge increases, so too does his ability to maximise the effect his powers have on the creatures of other dimensions he may be required to fight. At 3rd level, the trans-dime may add +2 to his manifester level whenever targeting a psychic entity with psi-powers.

Full Instruction: By the time he reaches 4th level, the trans-dime has become truly skilled at controlling psychic entities and forcing them to do his bidding. Even the most complicated instructions can now be given and will be obeyed. The limit for each instruction issued increases to twenty words.

Improved Control: The trans-dime's, mastery of his field is almost complete as he reaches 5th level. He is now able to extend his control over psychic entities in the real world for much greater lengths of time. The maximum time an entity can stay in the real world is increased to three hours. Each successive Control check to retain the services of the psychic entity for longer will now allow it to stay a further three hours in the real world instead of just one.

Experiments & Equipment

The physics and scientific laws of the psi-flux are poorly understood even by the most accomplished operatives within Psi-Division. The creation of technological devices to increase the ability of psi-talented characters is therefore far more an art than a science and many hold potential dangers of their own. The most famous of these items is the lethal psi-amplifier stored within Psi-Division's headquarters, Omar House, but psi-booster drugs commonly found on the street possess their own, not so hidden, dangers.

In addition to the equipment available legally or not, many of the larger corporations (and, some say, the Justice Department) are keen to perform a wide range of questionable experiments on citizens in an attempt to increase the normal level of psi-talent found in their operatives. Psykers can be big, if illegal, business within corporations as they have an undisputed advantage in the field of industrial espionage and the right placement of a powerful telepath can allow any flagging company to catch up and even overtake its rivals. The rivals in turn work hard to secure their own telepaths who are powerful enough to block and hunt down any spies. This is a secret war that has been fought between large businesses ever since rogue psykers started appearing in large numbers after the Atom War, and one the Justice Department tries hard to stamp out. Where millions or even billions of credits are involved, however, few citizens are willing to adhere to the Law.

This chapter takes a look at some of the psi-related equipment available to both judges and citizens on the streets, as well as adding a new prior life for citizens. Judges may now also call upon Exorcist Squads as a back-up unit.

Anti-Psi Drugs: First developed by the Justice Department to hinder the abilities of rogue psykers, anti-psi drugs can now be found on the black market by anyone seeking to negate psi-talent in another citizen.

Delivered by injection, a psi-talented character must make a Fortitude save at DC 20 or lose all power points for a period of one hour. Anti-psi drugs have no effect on characters without psi-talent.

Entity Amplification Scope: Many psychic entities possess the ability to make themselves invisible to human sight and even advanced scopes and infrared visors will be unable to detect them. Many psykers possess the second sight needed to follow and track such entities, but normal humans must rely on technological devices such as the entity amplification scope. Tuned into the frequencies of the psi-flux, this scope will permit any human to view an invisible psychic entity normally. The entity amplification scope has an effective range of 30 feet.

Null Shield: The null shield is nothing more than a sheet of one-inch thick, psychically charged plasteel, incredibly hard to produce, that will block almost any use of psi-talent. Each sheet is three feet square and several can be placed together to form an impenetrable shield around a vehicle, room or building. A single layer of null shield will automatically provide everything on the other side of it with Power Resistance 20. A double layer will automatically block any use of psi-talent from crossing it and will also completely prevent any psychic entity from moving through it. Null shields are opaque and cannot be made transparent by any means. The psi-brick used in Psi-Division's Omar House is effectively a triple layered null shield that prevents the leakage of any psi-talent known to man.

Psi-Amplifier: Potentially the most famous psychic-related device ever constructed, only one psi-amplifier is known to exist within Omar House, though it is likely that many large criminal organisations are working hard to build their own. The psi-amplifier is a huge device requiring awesome amounts of power. By laying inside, a psi-talented character may have his abilities magnified many times over though a terrible price is paid for its use – this boost comes at the expense of the character's own life force and any who enter the machine are doomed. A psi-amplifier will both quadruple a psi-talented character's manifester level and grant him unlimited power points. However, once inside, he cannot be disconnected without being killed and will only survive for a number of minutes equal to his Constitution ability score any-way. The psi-amplifier can therefore boost a character's psi-talent far beyond anything normally attainable by a human, but will do so at the cost of his life. The psi-amplifier has no effect on characters without psi-talent.

Psi-Booster Drugs: The complete reverse of anti-psi drugs, psi-boosters can temporarily increase a character's psi-talent to incredible levels, even though their minds were never meant for such abuse. A psi-talented character taking a dose of psi-booster drugs will immediately have his manifester level and power points total doubled. However, he must also make a Will save at DC 15 every 10 minutes while under the influence of psi-boosters, or sustain 1d6 points of temporary Constitution damage. This damage will be regained at the rate of one point for every full day of rest. Non-psi-talented characters taking psi-booster drugs will immediately gain 10 power points (not modified by their Charisma score) and one 0-level power randomly determined by the Games Master, though they must also test for Constitution damage as detailed before. Any character, psi-talented or not, taking psi-booster drugs more than once a day must make a Fortitude save at DC 18 or be immediately reduced to 0 hit points as the drugs ravage his system.

Psi-Focus: Using a combination of crystalline and advanced electronic technologies, psi-foci are a variety of instruments and devices designed to concentrate the use of any psi-talent and magnify their force. They are a common addition to the arsenal of equipment carried by exorcist judges when hunting psychic entities. All psi-foci are rated from +1 to +5, depending on the quality of construction and raw focussing power. When a power is manifested through a psi-focus (which may be done simply by the manifester holding or touching the device), this bonus is applied to all manifester checks to beat Power Resistance and to the DC of any saving throws required to resist the power. In addition, characters using the psi-focus to aid in the summon psychic entity power may use this bonus in both their Summoning and Control checks.

Psychic Battery: Similar in construction to a psi-focus, the psychic battery instead absorbs and

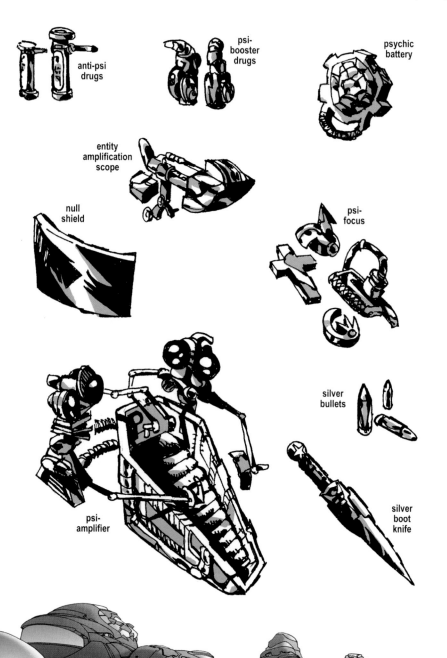

anti-psi drugs

psi-booster drugs

psychic battery

entity amplification scope

null shield

psi-focus

silver bullets

psi-amplifier

silver boot knife

Psi-Related Equipment

Item	Cost	Black Market Cost	Weight
Anti-Psi Drugs (1 dose)	250 cr.	900 cr.	-
Entity Amplification Scope	3,750 cr.	9,500 cr.	4 lb.
Null Shield (1 plate)	2,250 cr.	7,000 cr.	2 lb.
Psi-Amplifier	1,800,000 cr.	8,750,000 cr.	4,250 lb.
Psi-Booster Drugs (1 dose)	750 cr.	1,750 cr.	-
Psi-Focus +1	1,250 cr.	4,000 cr.	1 lb.
Psi-Focus +2	2,500 cr.	7,500 cr.	1 lb.
Psi-Focus +3	5,000 cr.	14,000 cr.	1 lb.
Psi-Focus +4	10,000 cr.	26,250 cr.	1 lb.
Psi-Focus +5	20,000 cr.	51,750 cr.	1 lb.
Psychic Battery (10)	2,750 cr.	8,000 cr.	1 lb.
Psychic Battery (25)	9,000 cr.	26,500 cr.	1 lb.
Psychic Battery (50)	19,950 cr.	59,000 cr.	1 lb.
Silver Boot Knife	1,250 cr.	-	1 lb.
Silver Bullets	X5	X6	*

* As original ammunition.

stores psychic energy until required by its owner. However, psychic batteries are a lot more difficult to construct and so demand a far higher price. Each psychic battery holds a number of power points indicated on the table above, which may be freely accessed by any psi-talented character simply by touching or holding the battery. They may be recharged by a psyker donating his psychic energy at a rate of 5 power points every hour.

Silver Boot Knife: Standard issue to all exorcist and psi-judges, a few Justice Department silver-bladed knives find their way on to the streets, while others are manufactured by specialist weaponsmiths who know only too well the potent edge such a weapon can grant when facing a psychic entity. Most perps, however, simply consider them a flash luxury of little value other than the credits they can demand. Any psychic entity struck by a silver weapon will suffer double damage, after any Damage Reduction has been taken into account.

Silver Bullets: With the exception of the shells granted to Psi-Division's exorcist judges, all silver bullets have to be custom-made and requests for them tend to raise a few eyebrows among most gunsmiths. Silver-tipped bullets can be made for any projectile-firing pistol or rifle and have a devastating effect upon psychic entities, though they are extremely expensive when compared to normal ammunition. Any psychic entity struck by a silver-tipped bullet will suffer double damage after any Damage Reduction has been taken into account.

Prior Life – Lab Rat

Players wishing to try a psi-talented citizen other than a rogue psyker may opt for the lab rat. The lab rat has been a victim all his life, having been kidnapped as an infant or born within a laboratory and subjected to the most mind-gruelling tests and drugs imaginable. A few of the city's mega-corporations and larger criminal organisations conduct such experiments in an effort to boost the psi-talent latent in many citizens. Most lab rats are doomed to die under the punishing experiments, but some manage to escape their enslavement and head out onto the streets where their fluctuating talent can be traded for both credits and protection. However, lab rats are inherently unstable, both in ability and personality, and so few ever manage to find peace of mind or contentment. Many are betrayed or handed over to the judges when their powers become too great or unstable for those protecting them to take further risks, no matter how well the lab rat has served them in the past.

† The lab rat is classed as having psi-talent, as described in Chapter 7 of the *Judge Dredd Rulebook*. He gains powers as shown on the rogue psyker powers table

on page 26 of the *Judge Dredd Rulebook*, though he may never become a specialist psyker.

† The lab rat's psychic stores are in a state of constant fluctuation, thanks to the remnants of drugs still floating through his system. He rolls 1d6 per psi-talented class level per day – this is his power points total for the next 24 hours. He gains no bonus power points for having a high Charisma score, though he must have a Charisma of at least 10 in order to be a lab rat.

† Though his power resources can never be relied upon, the lab rat is conditioned to channel his abilities in the most effective way possible. He always counts as having a manifester level one higher than normal for the purposes of manifester checks and the duration, etc; of powers.

† Having recently escaped his enslavement in some nameless laboratory, the lab rat has literally no possessions other than what he has been able to steal. He begins the game with just 500 credits.

Back Up Unit – Exorcist Squad

Back-up DC: 22
ETA: 5d6 minutes
Composition: 2 Exorcist judges on Lawmasters
The exorcist judges are among the most highly skilled operatives to be found within Psi-Division. Tasked with combating psychic entities rampaging through Mega-City One and demonic possessions, they are incredibly strong-willed and equipped to deal with almost any supernatural menace. Due to the unknown abilities of many of the creatures they will encounter, exorcist judges always work in pairs in order to both complement each other's abilities and for mutual protection against psychic assaults. There is a high mortality rate among the exorcist squads, due to the nature of the dangers they face, but there is never any shortage of volunteers willing to risk their lives for Mega-City One and defend its citizens against threats no one else is trained to deal with.

Sample Exorcist Judge

Psi-Judge 10 / Exorcist Judge 2: HD 12d8 (58); Spd 30 ft.; DV 23 (+13 Reflex); Attack +12/+7/+2 melee, or +13/+8/+3 ranged; Fort +12, Ref +13, Will +13; Str 10, Dex 13, Con 11, Int 12, Wis 13, Cha 16.
Skills and Feats: Concentration +3, Knowledge (law) +9, Knowledge (psi-talent) +13, Knowledge (psychic entities) +11, Psi-Scan +8, Ride +7, Sense Motive +9, Streetwise +7; Enhanced Power, Great Fortitude, Inner Strength, Iron Will, Lightning Reflexes, Nerves of Steel, Talented, Weapon Specialisation (boot knife), Weapon Focus (Lawgiver).
Power Points: 66.
Powers: 0-level: *detect psi-talent, detect psychic entity, inkling, mental shield, mind shield, missive, precognitive reflexes*; 1st level: *ectoplasmic shield, psychometry, second sight*; 2nd level: *detect thoughts, environmental psychometry, suggestion*; 3rd level: *danger sense, negate psi-talent*; 4th level: *dimensional anchor, dismiss*; 5th level: *psi-lash*.

Psychic Entities

The forces of other dimensions are not to be toyed with by mere mortals seeking to harness greater powers than they may control. This chapter contains entries for many psychic entities from other dimensions and other creatures that are capable of utilising psi-talent to achieve their own mysterious goals. It can be considered as an extension to the Creeps chapter of the *Judge Dredd Rulebook* and will enable Games Masters to greatly increase the diversity of opponents to set against his players.

Angel

Large Psychic Entity

Hit Dice: 22d12+110 (253 hp)
Initiative: +9 (+5 Dex, +4 Improved Initiative)
Speed: 50 ft., fly 150 ft.
DV: 30 (-1 size, +20 Reflex, +1 Dodge)
Damage Reduction: 20 (natural armour)
Attacks: Sword of light +35/+30/+25/+20/+15 melee
Damage: Sword of light 2d6+18/20
Face/Reach: 5 ft. by 5 ft./10 ft.
Special Attacks: Psi-talent
Special Qualities: Power Resistance 20, psychic entity
Saves: Fort +18, Ref +20, Will +20
Abilities: Str 28, Dex 20, Con 20, Int 23, Wis 25, Cha 25
Skills: Concentration +16, Escape Artist +30, Hide +26, Knowledge or Craft (any five) +28, Knowledge (psi-talent) +19, Listen +32, Move Silently +30, Search +30, Sense Motive +32, Spot 32
Feats: Dodge, Endurance, Improved Initiative, Lightning Reflexes, Luck of Grud, Mobility

Climate/Terrain: Any
Organisation: Solitary or pair
Advancement: 23-33 HD (large); 34-66 HD (huge)

It is a common belief that angels are benign creatures, interested in the welfare of mankind and looking upon his faults and foibles as a parent may a child. The truth could not be more different. Angels are psychic entities of awesome destructive power, capable of levelling entire sectors if allowed to roam free. While they ostensibly fight in the cause of justice and regularly battle across the dimensions against demons of all types, it is all too apparent that angels believe only in serving the greater good and will happily watch the destruction of entire cities, populations and worlds if it furthers their own ends. The exorcist judges of Psi-Division therefore view angels as no better than any other kind of demon and will pool their resources if ever one is detected entering the real world near Mega-City One.

angel

Angels appear as nine-foot-tall, winged humanoids with dazzling features, permanently surrounded by a bright nimbus of light. They have been witnessed wielding a wide range of different weaponry, though they all seem to function in much the same way as the sword of light depicted above. Angels are exceptionally powerful entities whose true purposes and motives may never be discerned by mankind. The death of an angel is a momentous event among the different dimensions and is bound to be avenged by other, more militant angels. Some believe that Judge Death himself once slew an angel as he travelled between dimensions and that their vendetta is the only thing that has stopped him from concentrating his full might against Mega-City One.

Combat

Once motivated to battle, angels are nigh on unstoppable. Rushing to engage its enemies, an angel will blast them with its awesome psychic powers before smashing them apart with its main weapon, the sword of light.

Psi-Talent: Angels are able to use the following powers at will – *banish, danger sense, detect psi-talent, dimensional anchor, mental shield, mind bomb, mind probe, negate psi-talent, sense psi-talent, tailor memory*, and *true sight*. They are able to use *epiphany, exorcise, mass domination, metafaculty, null psi-talent, turn psi-power*, and *psychic surgery* once per day. All powers are considered to be manifested by a 22nd level manifester.

Psychic Entity: Angels are psychic entities and so are immune to mind-influencing effects, poison, paralysis, stunning and disease. They are not subject to Arrest checks, critical hits, called shots, subdual damage, ability damage, energy drain, or death from massive damage. In addition, they suffer double damage from silver weapons.

Balruck

Large Psychic Entity

Hit Dice: 13d12+52 (137 hp)
Initiative: +5 (+1 Dex, +4 Improved Initiative)
Speed: 40 ft., fly 90 ft.
DV: 18 (-1 size, +9 Reflex)
Damage Reduction: 20 (natural armour)
Attacks: 2 Slams +19 melee
Damage: Slam 2d8 +7/20
Face/Reach: 5 ft. by 5 ft./10 ft.
Special Attacks: Body flames, psi-talent, terrifying appearance

Special Qualities: Death throes, Power Resistance 18, psychic entity
Saves: Fort +14, Ref +9, Will +13
Abilities: Str 25, Dex 13, Con 19, Int 20, Wis 20, Cha 16
Skills: Bluff +18, Concentration +19, Diplomacy +17, Hide +13, Knowledge (psi-talent) +13, Listen +28, Move Silently +13, Psi-Scan +21, Search +20, Sense Motive +20
Feats: Great Fortitude, Improved Bull Rush, Improved Critical (slam), Improved Initiative

Climate/Terrain: Any
Organisation: Solitary
Advancement: 14-19 HD (large); 20-39 HD (huge)

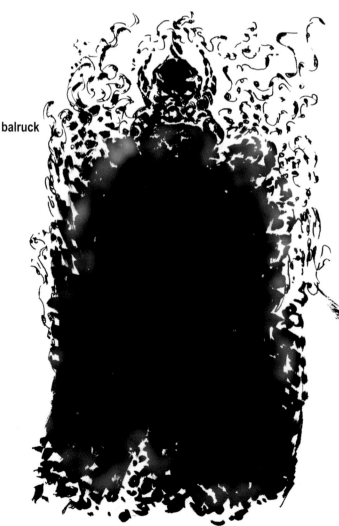

balruck

It is not clear whether the balruck is an individual demon, or is part of an entire race of such psychic entities. What is apparent is that when a balruck breaks through into the real world, mankind itself may be in jeopardy. The balruck is a thing of nightmare, standing over twelve feet tall and wreathed in flame, its demonically twisted features are utterly alien and promise doom to any unfortunate enough to look upon them. Its hard and toughened skin is the deepest black, and is often enveloped in huge bat-like wings, granting yet another layer of defence that can withstand even heavy artillery shells.

Among the greatest of all known demons, the balruck rules entire dimensions, but is consumed by an all-encompassing greed to dominate the real world and enslave all of mankind. There are few psykers capable of standing up to the assault of a balruck, no matter what their level of mastery, and perhaps the only viable response to an intrusion upon the real world is massed laser and missile fire, as well as prayers that such firepower will simply drive the creature away.

Combat

The balruck will display no patience in combat, seeking to utterly destroy as many enemies as possible within the shortest period of time. It will use a combination of psychic and melee attacks to sweep aside opponents, with no pretence at subtlety or advanced tactics. If forced to retreat, the balruck will rely more upon its psi-talent and will start to summon other psychic entities to join the battle.

Body Flames: The balruck is permanently enshrouded in red hot flames. These flames grant the demon immunity to all fire damage, as well as cause 4d8 points of fire damage to any creature grappling the balruck.
Death Throes: When slain, the balruck will explode in a brilliant burst of psychokinetic activity. Everything within 100 ft. will automatically be dealt 50 points of fire damage though a Reflex save (DC 20) will halve this.
Psi-Talent: The balruck is able to use the following powers at will – *control flames, detect psi-talent, dimensional anchor, ectoplasmic attack, fire of retribution, mental shield, mind bomb, mind probe, negate psi-talent, sense psi-talent, summon psychic entity* and *undeath*. They are able to use *crushing force, exorcise, flaming shroud, null psi-talent, rolling fire, spontaneous combustion* and *tempest of fire* once per day. All powers are considered to be manifested by a 13th level manifester.

Psychic Entity: The balruck is a psychic entity and so is immune to mind-influencing effects, poison, paralysis, stunning and disease. It is not subject to Arrest checks, critical hits, called shots, subdual damage, ability damage, energy drain, or death from massive damage. In addition, it suffers double damage from silver weapons.
Terrifying Appearance: The balruck is terrifying to behold and many creatures simply flee from its presence, rather than risk its wrath. Any living creature seeing the balruck must make a Will save (DC 20) or immediately flee the area in fear, at the greatest possible speed, for 3d6 rounds. If the save is successful, the creature will never suffer from the effects of the balruck's terrifying appearance again.

Gargarax

Medium Psychic Entity

Hit Dice: 12d12+39 (117 hp)
Initiative: +1 (+1 Dex)
Speed: 40 ft.
DV: 19 (+9 Reflex)
Damage Reduction: 4 (natural armour)
Attacks: Slam +14/+9/+4 melee
Damage: Slam 2d6+2/4
Face/Reach: 5 ft. by 5 ft./5 ft.
Special Attacks: Improved possession, psi-talent
Special Qualities: Power Resistance 8, psychic entity
Saves: Fort +11, Ref +9, Will +10
Abilities: Str 14, Dex 12, Con 16, Int 14, Wis 15, Cha 18
Skills: Climb +6, Escape Artist +7, Hide +7, Intuit Direction +3, Jump +6, Listen +7, Move Silently +7, Search +6, Spot +7
Feats: Run, Toughness, Weapon Focus (slam)

Climate/Terrain: Any
Organisation: Solitary
Advancement: None (unique)

Gargarax was a powerful entity that Psi-Judge Anderson encountered while investigating the possession of a juve in Ed Poe block. Fooling a witch coven in the same block, the demon managed to gain access to the real world and possessed a young juve, Hammy Blish, in an elaborate attempt to forge a permanent opening to his own dimension. This accomplished, he would lead a horde of demonkin into the real world to conquer Mega-City One and enslave its population. Anderson was able to travel to Gargarax's home dimension and defeat the demon on his own turf, though she was forced to kill the conduit, Hammy, in order to stop the demonic assault upon her city.

gargarax

Gargarax had an immensely strong will and was a potent psyker. He could dominate any mortal in a very short space of time and was skilled at possession. Though Gargarax is now dead, thanks to Anderson's heroic efforts, Games Masters may like to use the demon as an example of the countless fiends that constantly plot their entry to the real world.

Combat

Gargarax is a canny demon who knows the extent of his own powers but values immortality a great deal more than taking risks. He will seek to ambush his victims wherever possible, either possessing them with his incredible mental strength or employing his psi-talent to quickly dispatch any obstacle to his plans.

Improved Possession: Gargarax has an incredibly strong will and specialises in possessing weaker minds. Any creature trying to resist Gargarax possessing them suffers a –4 circumstance penalty to their Will save.

Psi-Talent: Gargarax is 3rd level manifester with 11 power points the following powers – 0-level: *detect psi-talent, incinerating finger*; 1st level: *sense living*.

Psychic Entity: Gargarax is a psychic entity and so is immune to mind-influencing effects, poison, paralysis, stunning and disease. He is not subject to Arrest checks, critical hits, called shots, subdual damage, ability damage, energy drain, or death from massive damage. In addition, he suffers double damage from silver weapons.

Ghost

Ghosts are, perhaps, the most common type of psychic entity any dimensionalist or exorcist judge will encounter. What happens to the human soul after death has never been fully understood, but it is clear that a transference of energies does indeed take place, perhaps sending the deceased's consciousness to another dimension for eternity. Sometimes, however, something goes wrong with this process and, for whatever reason, a spirit or shadow of the original person remains in the real world. Myth and legend describe haunted spirits not being able to rest until their death has been avenged or some wrong they committed in life has finally been righted, and the Exorcist Squad of Psi-Division has many confirmed cases of ghosts resisting all attempts to banish them to another dimension until they are at peace. This often takes a great deal of research on the part of exorcist judges to discover who the ghost actually is and what happened at their time of death.

These psychic entities are often tied to a particular location that has some meaning to their death, and most seem unable to travel more than half a mile or so from this point. By and large, ghosts rarely trouble the living as they seek to put right whatever ties them to the real world but when they do interfere, they can be terrifying foes. The mere touch of a ghost is said to be able to chill a man to the bone, and their incorporeal nature usually defeats any mundane defence.

'Ghost' is a template that can be added to any living creature who has been killed, regardless of race or location. All of the creature's statistics and abilities remain unchanged, except as noted below.

Hit Dice: Increase to d12.
Speed: Fly 60 ft.

Entities

ghost

The ghost may take on a terrifying appearance as a free action. Any living creature witnessing this must make a Will save (DC 10 + ghost's Hit Dice) or immediately flee the area in fear, at the greatest possible speed, for 2d4 rounds. If the save is successful, the creature will never suffer from the effects of the ghost's terrifying apparition again.

Special Qualities

Incorporeal: Ghosts are completely unsubstantial and, as such, can only be harmed by other psychic entities or psi-powers. They can pass through any solid object at will.
Invisible: Ghosts can turn themselves invisible at will as a free action. Only other psychic entities and characters with psi-talent manifesting certain powers (such as *second sight* or *true sight*) can view invisible ghosts. Ghosts gain a +2 bonus to all attack rolls while invisible and are considered to have total concealment themselves against enemies.
Power Resistance: Ghosts gain Power Resistance 6 + their Hit Dice.
Psychic Entity: Ghosts are psychic entities and so are immune to mind-influencing effects, poison, paralysis, stunning and disease. They are not subject to Arrest checks, critical hits, called shots, subdual damage, ability damage, energy drain, or death from massive damage. In addition, they suffer double damage from silver weapons.
Repeater: Most ghosts are known as 'repeaters' by exorcist judges – even if they can be destroyed, they will inevitably return within 1d4 days unless their ties to the real world can be severed (usually by completing some task the ghost is unable to perform for itself).

Abilities: The ghost has no Strength or Constitution score, but receives a +4 bonus to its Charisma.
Skills: Ghosts receive a +8 circumstance bonus to all Hide checks.
Psi-Talent: A ghost will possess any psi-talent it originally had in life.

Climate/Terrain: Any.
Organisation: Solitary.
Advancement: None. Ghosts are trapped both in the real world and in time, and so can never advance.

Ghoul

Medium Psychic Entity

Hit Dice: 2d12+4 (17 hp)
Initiative: +2 (+2 Dex)
Speed: 40 ft.

Attacks: Ghosts lose any attacks they had previously and instead have a death touch attack. A death touch will ignore any Damage Reduction but affects only living creatures. Any living creature struck by a death touch must make a Fortitude save (DC 10 + ghost's Hit Dice) or immediately suffer 1d6 points of permanent damage to its Strength, Dexterity and Constitution ability scores. This damage can only be negated by *psychic surgery*.

Special Attacks

Possession: Ghosts who possess 10 or more Hit Dice are able to possess other living creatures, as described on p50.
Terrifying Apparition: Ghosts can change their appearance from an insubstantial representation of how they looked in their previous life, to an angry and decaying spirit guaranteed to quail the strongest of hearts.

DV: 12 (+2 Reflex)

Damage Reduction: 6 (natural armour)

Attacks: Bite +3 melee; 2 claws +0 melee

Damage: Bite 1d8+1/8 and paralysis; claw 1d6-1/4

Face/Reach: 5 ft. by 5 ft./5 ft.

Special Attacks: Paralysis

Special Qualities: Power Resistance 8, psychic entity, *sense living*

Saves: Fort +2, Ref +2, Will +5

Abilities: Str 13, Dex 15, Con 14, Int 13, Wis 14, Cha 16

Skills: Climb +6, Escape Artist +7, Hide +7, Intuit Direction +3, Jump +6, Listen +7, Move Silently +7, Search +6, Spot +7

Feats: Multiattack, Weapon Focus (bite)

ghoul

Climate/Terrain: Any land or underground

Organisation: Solitary or pack (2-40)

Advancement: 3-4 HD (medium)

Little is known about the ghouls of the other dimensions but whenever they break into the real world, they do so with an utter desire to feast upon the souls and flesh of all living creatures. Their total single-mindedness to destroy all life but their own causes ghouls to gather in great packs at any weak spot between dimensions, waiting for the chance to launch a fresh assault.

A ghoul's true form of an emaciated humanoid belies its keen intellect and low cunning, both of which it will employ to harvest its prey. Veteran operatives of the Exorcist Squad in the Justice Department's Psi-Division often mistakenly believe ghouls to be cowards at heart, for a strong display of force will often cause even large packs of them to scatter and run. However, such complacency has proved lethal in the past as the pack regroups and launches a fresh attack from a completely new direction. Ghouls are capable of employing quite advanced tactics against their prey, though they usually eschew any available weaponry in favour of their lightning speed, razor sharp claws and paralysing bite. These creatures have a tendency to revert to their basest natures when involved in combat, often ignoring enemies to feast upon the still living, but paralysed, body of a downed victim.

Combat

Ghouls are skilful and cunning combatants, attempting to ambush and surprise their prey whenever possible in order to gain victory and an easy meal. They rarely fight to the death and will quickly retreat if faced with heavy resistance and mounting losses.

Paralysis: Any living creature taking damage from a ghoul's bite must immediately succeed at a Fortitude save (DC 14) or be paralysed for 1d10 minutes, unable to perform any action (though psi-talent may still be manifested).

Psychic Entity: Ghouls are psychic entities and so are immune to mind-influencing effects, poison, paralysis, stunning and disease. They are not subject to Arrest checks, critical hits, called shots, subdual damage, ability damage, energy drain, or death from massive damage. In addition, they suffer double damage from silver weapons.

Sense Living: Ghouls can manifest *sense living* at will, as if they were 2nd level manifesters.

Gremlin

Tiny Psychic Entity

gremlins

Hit Dice: 1d12+3 (10 hp)
Initiative: +1 (+1 Dex)
Speed: 30 ft.
DV: 13 (+2 size, +1 Reflex)
Damage Reduction: 2 (natural armour)
Attacks: Bite +1 melee
Damage: Bite 1d8-1/2
Face/Reach: 2 ½ ft. by 2 ½ ft./2 ½ ft.
Special Qualities: Psychic entity
Saves: Fort +0, Ref +1, Will +1
Abilities: Str 8, Dex 13, Con 11, Int 6, Wis 8, Cha 7
Skills: Hide +5, Listen +3, Move Silently +5, Search +1, Spot +2
Feats: Toughness

Climate/Terrain: Any land or underground
Organisation: Pack (10-100) or horde (100-1,000)*
Advancement: 3-4 HD (medium)

The term gremlin was coined within the Exorcist Squad for a number of minor psychic entities that remain trapped within their own dimensions. It quickly becomes apparent that, despite the humour in the name, there is nothing funny about an attack of gremlins upon the real world. Many seem closely related to ghouls and are often seen in their company, forced ahead of the larger psychic entities to spearhead assaults into the real world whenever summoned by foolish psykers or the barriers between dimensions weaken sufficiently to make their own access.

Gremlins are simple psychic entities that ghouls find easy to bully and cajole into fulfilling whatever tasks they wish to avoid doing themselves. Taking the form of small and repugnant humanoids, gremlins are completely hairless, have grey skin and huge mouths in which they brandish their main weapon – six inch long fangs capable of slicing a man apart within seconds. They are extremely hardy little psychic entities for their size and can withstand a great deal of punishment before being slain.

* The Games Master may prefer to use the mass combat rules within *The Rookie's Guide to Block Wars* to play out scenarios involving larger gremlin invasions upon the real world.

Combat

Gremlins are simple psychic entities often forced into battle by other, tougher creatures whom they fear. Their attacks are based purely on weight of numbers and though many may fall as they close range on an enemy, there are usually enough to succeed in overcoming any defence.

Psychic Entity: Gremlins are psychic entities and so are immune to mind-influencing effects, poison, paralysis, stunning and disease. They are not subject to Arrest checks, critical hits, called shots, subdual damage, ability damage, energy drain, or death from massive damage. In addition, they suffer double damage from silver weapons.

Poltergeist

Medium Psychic Entity

Hit Dice: 8d12 (52 hp)
Initiative: -1 (Dex)
Speed: 30 ft.
DV: 15 (+5 Reflex)
Damage Reduction: 12 (natural armour)
Attacks: None

Damage: None
Face/Reach: 5 ft. by 5 ft./5 ft.
Special Attacks: Telekinetic psi-talent
Special Qualities: Incorporeal, Power Resistance 10, psychic entity
Saves: Fort +2, Ref +5, Will +7
Abilities: Str -, Dex 17, Con –, Int 2, Wis 12, Cha 14
Skills: Hide +8, Listen +7, Search +3, Spot +6
Feats: Alertness, Blind-Fight

Climate/Terrain: Any land or underground
Organisation: Solitary
Advancement: 9-10 HD (medium)

Often confused with ghosts, poltergeists are actually small pockets of psychic energy that leak through from other dimensions or pool in the real world, gaining a small measure of consciousness and sense of self. Poltergeists can become manifest at any location where a great deal of psychic activity has taken place or where other psychic entities have broken free into the real world. Others are born from the undisciplined use of psi-talent by powerful juve psykers. A few are created by foolish psykers who seek to summon psychic entities directly into the real world to fulfil their own devious and selfish goals. Poltergeists are usually bound to a specific location and are unable to move more than a few feet from their place of origin.

Poltergeists are only able to affect the real world through the use of their innate psi-talent, using telekinetic force to move and hurl objects at any target that antagonises them. Though invisible to normal sight, beings capable of viewing poltergeists perceive them as formless clouds that constantly swirl, expand and contract as the entity uses its powers.

poltergeist

Combat

Poltergeists are essentially mindless entities bent on causing chaos wherever they manifest themselves. Though they may lie dormant for weeks or even months, when roused they attack with all the telekinetic powers at their disposal.

Incorporeal: Poltergeists are completely unsubstantial and, as such, can only be harmed by other psychic entities or psi-powers. They can pass through any solid object at will.

Psychic Entity: Poltergeists are psychic entities and so are immune to mind-influencing effects, poison, paralysis, stunning and disease. They are not subject to Arrest checks, critical hits, called shots, subdual damage, ability damage, energy drain, or death from massive damage. In addition, they suffer double damage from silver weapons.

Telekinetic Psi-Talent: Poltergeists are able to use the following powers at will – *concussion*, *minor telekinesis* and *telekinesis*. They are able to use *aggressive telekinesis*, *control body* and *greater telekinesis* once per day. All powers are considered to be manifested by an 8th level manifester.

Entities

Skull Child

Small Psychic Entity

Hit Dice: 4d12 (26 hp)
Initiative: +2 (+2 Dex)
Speed: 20 ft.
DV: 14 (+1 size, +3 Reflex)
Damage Reduction: 0
Attacks: 2 claws +3 melee; or bite –2 melee
Damage: 2 claws 1d3/8; or bite 1d4/6 and 1d4 Con
Face/Reach: 2 ½ ft. by 2 ½ ft./2 ½ ft.
Special Attacks: Constitution damage, terrifying gaze
Special Qualities: Create skull child, masquerade, Power Resistance 6, psychic entity
Saves: Fort +1, Ref +3, Will +4
Abilities: Str 10, Dex 15, Con 10, Int 8, Wis 11, Cha 11
Skills: Climb +4, Hide +8, Listen +7, Move Silently +6, Search +3, Spot +6
Feats: Alertness, Blind-Fight

skull
child

Climate/Terrain: Any land or underground
Organisation: Solitary or gang (2-5)
Advancement: 3-6 HD (Small)

Skull children are small and pathetic, but incredibly sadistic, psychic entities, often spoken of in folklore and myth. Entering the real world from their own dark dimension, they prey upon humans to draw sustenance and create more of their own kind. By day, a skull child is virtually indiscernible from any juve of its size and apparent age. They appear as happy, playful youngsters who mix with other, more normal juves. At night, however, their true demeanour becomes all too apparent for as the sun sinks below the horizon, the flesh retreats from the head of a skull child, revealing a bare skull with blazing eye sockets and sharp, needle-like teeth. The rest of their diminutive bodies become putrid and rotten. At night, skull children feed on the life force of other living creatures, draining the essence of their victims. A solitary skull child will often pose as a young orphan in order to be taken in by well-meaning and unsuspecting citizens, while others may operate as gangs of destitute juves in Mega-City One.

A skull child will seek to insinuate itself into gangs of juves, camouflaging itself amongst the living and slowly preying upon them, one by one. It is not known whether these psychic entities prefer to stalk juves in order to create more of their own kind or simply because they are far easier targets.

Combat

Skull children prefer to avoid combat if possible, all too aware that their small forms are unsuited to battle. When forced to fight, however, they attack with bony claws and a vicious bite.

Constitution Damage: If the bite of a skull child causes damage, it will also deal 1d4 points of permanent Constitution damage unless the victim makes a Fortitude save (DC 12). Only *psychic surgery* can repair this damage.
Create Spawn: If a skull child manages to slay a juve by draining its Constitution to 0, the unlucky victim will rise once more in one day as a free-willed skull child. An *exorcise* cast on the body before that time will cease the transformation, as will the body being taken to Resyk. Adults will simply be slain by this Constitution drain and will not rise as a skull child.
Terrifying Gaze: Any living creature that meets the gaze of a skull child must make a Will save (DC 12) or be

shaken for 1d4 rounds. Shaken creatures suffer a –2 morale penalty on all saving throws, attack and damage roll. Creatures of more than 5 character levels or Hit Dice are immune to this effect.

Masquerade: Between the hours of dawn and dusk, it is impossible to tell a skull child apart from another, more normal, juve. Any form of detection, such as *aura sight* or *detect psychic entity* will reveal nothing out of the ordinary. *True sight* will show a dark haze around the skull child during the day but nothing more.

Psychic Entity: Skull children are psychic entities and so are immune to mind-influencing effects, poison, paralysis, stunning and disease. They are not subject to Arrest checks, critical hits, called shots, subdual damage, ability damage, energy drain, or death from massive damage. In addition, they suffer double damage from silver weapons.

Succubus

Medium Psychic Entity

Hit Dice: 6d12 (39 hp)
Initiative: +5 (+1 Dex, +4 Improved Initiative)
Speed: 30 ft., fly 90 ft.
DV: 16 (+6 Reflex)
Damage Reduction: 12 (natural armour)
Attacks: 2 claws +7 melee
Damage: 2 claws 1d12+1/12
Face/Reach: 5 ft. by 5 ft./5 ft.
Special Attacks: Ecstatic kiss, psi-talent
Special Qualities: Power Resistance 12, psychic entity
Saves: Fort +6, Ref +6, Will +7
Abilities: Str 13, Dex 13, Con 13 Int 16, Wis 14, Cha 20
Skills: Bluff +11, Concentration +7, Disguise +11, Escape Artist +7, Hide +7, Knowledge (psi-talent) +9, Listen +16, Move Silently +7, Ride +7, Search +9, Spot +16
Feats: Improved Initiative, Lightning Reflexes

Climate/Terrain: Any
Organisation: Solitary
Advancement: 7-12 HD (medium)

Succubi are creatures of legend, usually taking the form of highly attractive human women intent on bringing about the moral downfall of all good and noble men. In actual fact, succubi are lethal demons from another dimension who delight in preying on any human and are capable of assuming either male or female form at will. Whatever their appearance, succubi will always have brilliant and glowing eyes, flawless skin and a perfect build, though their true nature is belied by large, bat-like wings. Upon entering the real world, a succubus will tempt and pervert any human it comes across, coaxing them into sexual contact where the victim's very life essence will be drained in acts of pure ecstasy and pleasure. Few humans are truly strong-willed enough to resist the lures of a succubus and many will willingly lay down their lives in defending one that has already dominated them. Most succubi are well aware of the judges in Mega-City One, and some target such defenders of humanity above all others, delighting in their ability to corrupt even a man who has dedicated his entire life to the defence of his fellow citizens.

Combat
Succubi are surprisingly adept at combat and are fully capable of tearing a man's head off with their bare hands when enraged. However, these demons prefer to work on

succubi

a much more subtle level, and will use the full weight of their sensuous bodies and incredible psychic powers to lure victims to them and turn groups of enemies upon each other.

Ecstatic Kiss: Through the use of their potent psi-talent, succubi are capable of convincing many mortal creatures to willingly kiss them. However, the kiss of a succubus, while a source of the most intense pleasure imaginable, is also the method by which the demon drains the life essence of its prey. Any mortal willingly kissing a succubus (a full round action for both man and demon) must make a Fortitude save (DC 18) or immediately lose a character level. The character will have his experience point total reduced to the minimum required for his new, lower level and will lose all benefits gained such as hit points, feats, class features and so on. This loss is permanent and may only be reversed by *psychic surgery*. If a succubus reduces a character to 0 level through the ecstatic kiss, the character will be immediately slain and the succubus will automatically be healed of any damage it has suffered.

Psi-Talent: Succubi are 12th level manifesters with 72 power points and the following powers – 0-level: *daze, detect psi-talent, empathy, mental shield, missive*; 1st level: *attraction & aversion, conceal thoughts, enrapture*; 2nd level: *settle, suggestion*; 3rd level: *danger sense, fabricated reality*; 4th level: *domination, tailor memory*; 5th level: *mind probe*.

Psychic Entity: Succubi are psychic entities and so are immune to mind-influencing effects, poison, paralysis, stunning and disease. They are not subject to Arrest checks, critical hits, called shots, subdual damage, ability damage, energy drain, or death from massive damage. In addition, they suffer double damage from silver weapons.

Vampire

Having been a staple of many horror-vids over the decades, vampires are perhaps the most well known psychic entity – even the most unsophisticated citizen knows a vampyre feeds off blood, needs a coffin to sleep in during the day and that they can be warded off with garlic. It is unfortunate that most citizens also believe that vampires simply do not exist and are merely the product of vid-producers with little real imagination.

Exorcist judges within Psi-Division, however, have some inkling of the truth. While vampires are, by and large, incredibly rare anywhere in the real world, they are all

vampire

too real and must be terminated with extreme prejudice whenever found, for they are capable of wiping out entire populations given time. Vampires are unusual psychic entities in that the real world is their home dimension and so many of the tools and tactics employed by exorcist judges simply do not work. They are supernaturally fast, can shrug off incredible amounts of damage without registering pain and are utterly lethal if allowed to close range. Possessing inhuman strength, vampires can rend a man apart in seconds and their famous bite will drain any living creature of its life, causing it to rise as another vampyre. In this way, vampyres can almost seem like an infection if allowed to spread in a mega-city, as greater numbers are created whenever they strike at the citizen population.

Vampires possess few of the weaknesses the horror-vids are keen to grant them and those who battle against these fiends with this false knowledge are doomed. It can prove incredibly difficult to completely destroy even a relatively weak vampire and many exorcist judges have met their end attempting to do so.

'Vampire' is a template that can be added to any living creature. All of the creature's statistics and abilities remain unchanged, except as noted below.

Hit Dice: Increase to d12.
Speed: Double original creature's.
Damage Reduction: Vampires gain a natural Damage Reduction of 15.
Attacks: Vampires retain all attacks possessed by the original creature. In addition, they also gain a slam attack.
Damage: Vampyres will cause damage with their slam attack based on their size, as shown on the table below.

Size	Damage
Fine	1
Diminutive	1d2
Tiny	1d3
Small	1d4
Medium-size	1d6
Large	1d8
Huge	2d6
Gargantuan	2d8
Colossal	4d6

Special Attacks

Blood Sucker: Any vampyre who succeeds in a Grapple check may automatically bite its victim and begin to drain its blood. The victim will immediately lose 1d6 points of Constitution permanently. This loss can only be reversed through the use of *psychic surgery*. Any victim reduced to 0 Constitution will automatically die and rise up as another vampyre within 1d6 hours. The new vampyre will be subservient to the original as if *thrall* had been manifested upon it. A vampyre can have as many *thrall* vampyres under its control as it is able to raise.
Home Dimension: The home dimension of any vampyre will be the one in which it was created, which will usually be the real world. As such, vampyres are immune to the effects of *banish*, *dismiss* and *exorcise* psi-powers, and will merely be forced back 10 ft. away from the manifester if they are attempted. However, vampyres cannot be summoned and are also unable to possess any creature, regardless of how many Hit Dice they have.
Mind Control: Vampyres can manifest *domination* and *suggestion* at will, as if they were 12th level manifesters, simply by looking into a victim's eyes. This ability has a range of 30 ft.

Special Qualities

Electricity Resistance: Vampyres gain Electricity Resistance 12.
Power Resistance: Vampyres gain Power Resistance 10 + their Hit Dice.
Psychic Entity: Vampyres are psychic entities and so are immune to mind-influencing effects, poison, paralysis, stunning and disease. They are not subject to Arrest checks, critical hits, called shots, subdual damage, ability damage, energy drain, or death from massive damage. In addition, they suffer double damage from silver weapons.
Tough to Kill: Victims soon learn that vampyres are incredibly hard creatures to kill. A vampyre will automatically heal 5 points of damage every round. If reduced to 0 hit points, the vampyre will fall comatose and appear dead, but will rise again with full hit points within 1d6 hours. Only a wooden stake through the heart will permanently kill a vampyre and it must be held immobile or be comatose for this to be attempted.

Abilities: The vampyre receives a +8 bonus to its Strength, +6 to its Dexterity, +6 to its Constitution, +2 to its Intelligence, +4 to its Wisdom and +4 to its Charisma ability scores.
Skills: Ghosts receive a +8 circumstance bonus to all Hide, Listen, Move Silently, Search and Spot checks.

IT HAD STARTED WITH HIS SCREAM —

Feats: Vampyres gain the following feats; Alertness, Improved Initiative, and Lightning Reflexes.
Psi-Talent: A vampyre will possess any psi-talent it originally had in life.

Climate/Terrain: Any.
Organisation: Solitary, pair or gang (3-10).
Advancement: By character class.

Wraith

Medium Psychic Entity

Hit Dice: 7d12 (38 hp)
Initiative: +7 (+3 Dex, +4 Improved Initiative)
Speed: Fly 60 ft.
DV: 14 (+4 Reflex)
Damage Reduction: 2 (natural armour)
Attacks: Touch +5 melee
Damage: Touch 1d4/20 and 1d6 Con drain
Face/Reach: 5 ft. by 5 ft./5 ft.
Special Attacks: Constitution damage, create wraith
Special Qualities: Daylight powerlessness, incorporeal, Power Resistance 10, psychic entity, unnatural aura
Saves: Fort +1, Ref +4, Will +6
Abilities: Str -, Dex 16, Con –, Int 14, Wis 14, Cha 15
Skills: Concentration +10, Hide +11, Intimidate +10, Listen +12, Search +10, Sense Motive +8, Spot +12
Feats: Alertness, Blind-Fight, Combat Reflexes, Improved Initiative

Climate/Terrain: Mega-City One, the Cursed Earth or the Undercity
Organisation: Solitary or gang (2-5)
Advancement: 8-12 HD (medium)

Wraiths are insubstantial but extremely powerful creatures from another dimension, whose touch is said to be death itself. Taking the appearance of dark, formless shadows, they often seem humanoid in shape with dark red, piercing eyes. It is said by those who possess knowledge of other dimensions that wraiths are the souls of the damned trapped between the real world and the afterlife as payment for their sins. Raging against their fate, wraiths are utterly lethal to any living creature, and seek to break into the real world to enact their revenge at any opportunity.

Combat

Wraiths are fast-moving shadows in combat, striking from the darkness whenever they can and relying on their lethal touch to slay all living creatures.

Constitution Damage: Any living creature hit by a wraith's touch attack must make a successful Fortitude save (DC 14) or suffer 1d6 points of permanent Constitution damage. Only *psychic surgery* can repair this damage.
Create Wraith: Wraiths can enslave the souls of their victims and forge them into their own image. Any living creature killed by a wraith will become a wraith itself in 1d6 rounds. They will be completely enslaved and subservient to the wraith that created them.
Daylight Powerlessness: Natural sunlight renders wraiths completely powerless and they flee from it whenever able.
Incorporeal: Wraiths are completely unsubstantial and,

wraith

as such, can only be harmed by other psychic entities or psi-powers. They can pass through any solid object at will.

Psychic Entity: Wraiths are psychic entities and so are immune to mind-influencing effects, poison, paralysis, stunning and disease. They are not subject to Arrest checks, critical hits, called shots, subdual damage, ability damage, energy drain, or death from massive damage. In addition, they suffer double damage from silver weapons.

Unnatural Aura: Wild and domestic animals and beasts can sense the presence of a wraith at a distance of 30 feet. They will not willingly approach a wraith and will attempt to flee if possible.

Zombie

Medium Undead

Hit Dice: 2d12+3 (16 hp)
Initiative: -1 (Dex)
Speed: 30 ft.
DV: 9 (-1 Reflex)
Damage Reduction: 8 (natural armour)
Attacks: Slam +2 melee
Damage: Slam 1d8+1/2
Face/Reach: 5 ft. by 5 ft./5 ft.
Special Qualities: Undead, partial actions only
Saves: Fort +0, Ref -1, Will +3
Abilities: Str 13, Dex 8, Con 10, Int -, Wis 10, Cha 1
Feats: Toughness

Climate/Terrain: Mega-City One, the Cursed Earth or the Undercity
Organisation: Solitary or mob (2-20)
Advancement: 3-5 HD (medium); 6-10 HD (large)

Zombies are literally the walking dead, animated corpses that possess just a spark of their previous life. They shuffle around, targeting any living creature unless controlled by a powerful psyker, who can direct them to perform simple tasks. Zombies decay rapidly and are horrific to look upon, with rotting clothes and flesh hanging off their bones as they shamble around to club any living creature to death. These creatures can be created by psykers using the *undeath* power, or may arise naturally in areas of great psychic disturbance.

Combat

Zombies are unsophisticated in combat and are unlikely to be able to succeed in any sort of battle plan or

advanced tactics, even if controlled. They aim to simply pummel their enemies to death with their fists, advancing in a slow wave that will gradually overcome any defences.

Partial Actions Only: Zombies are very slow and may only perform partial actions. As such, they can move or attack, but not both unless they charge (which will be considered a partial charge).

Undead: Immune to mind-influencing effects, poison, paralysis, stunning and disease. Not subject to critical hits, called shots, subdual damage, ability damage, energy drain, or death from massive damage. In addition, they automatically pass all Arrest checks.

zombie

Rules Summary

General Psi-Powers

0-Level

Daze - Character loses next action.*
Detect Psi-Talent - Detect the presence of psi-activity.*
Empathy - Know subject's surface emotions.*
Inkling - 50% likely to know if an intended action is good or bad.*
Mental Shield – Grants Damage Reduction against powers.
Mental Sting – Deal 1d6 points of damage to a subject.*
Mind Shield - Subject gains Power Resistance.*
Missive - Send a one-way telepathic message to subject.*

1st Level

Conceal Thoughts - Conceal motives.*
Demoralise - Foes suffer –1 penalty on some actions.*
Psychometry - Know about an object's past.*
Sense Living - Determines the precise locations of living creatures.
Telempathic Projection - Modify subject's emotions.*

2nd Level

Augury - Learn if an intended action will be good or bad.*
Clairvoyance - Hear or see at a distance.*
Detect Thoughts - Detect subject's surface thoughts.*
Environmental Psychometry - Find out about an area's past.*
Settle - Calms dangerous animals and beasts.

3rd Level

Blanking - Hides subject from psi-powers and psi scanning.*
Danger Sense - Gain a +4 bonus against traps.*
Negate Psi-Talent - Nullifies other powers as they take effect.
Psi Scan - See subject from a distance.*
Schism - Splits mind into two independently functional parts.*

4th Level

Aura Sight - Read things in other's auras.*
Detect Psi Scanning - Know when others psi scan you.*
Divination - Provides specific advice for proposed actions.*
Implant False Memory - False memory implanted in subject.*

5th Level

Gestalt - Links minds to magnify powers.
Mind Probe - Discover the subject's secret thoughts.*
Physical Adaptation - Manifester can resist extremes of environment.
Psi Lash - Unleashes a blast of psychic energy into a target's mind.*
Sense Psi-Talent - Sense powers and psi effects.*

6th Level

Aura Alteration - Subject seems to be something it is not.*
Null Psi-Talent - Creates a psychic free zone.
Mind Switch - Switch minds with another.*
Precognition - More in-depth than divination.*

7th Level

Emulate Power – Manifests any other power.
Insanity - Subject is permanently confused.*
Mind Bomb - Mental scream that deals 9d6 damage to all within 15 ft.*
Turn Psi-Power - Rebounds powers back on to other manifesters.

8th Level

Foresight - Senses warning of impending danger.*
Mind Blank - Subject immune to mental/emotional effects and psi scanning.*

9th Level

Metafaculty - Subject cannot hide name or location.*

Dimensionalist Psi-Powers

0 Level

Detect Psychic Entity - Reveals all psychic entities in the area.
Ghostly Whispers - Distracts an enemy with incoherent babble.

1st Level

Ectoplasmic Shield - Grants subject Damage Reduction 10.
Second Sight - View invisible psychic entities.
Undeath - Turns a corpse into a zombie.

2nd Level

Evil Eye - Curses a subject, doing 1 point of Charisma damage.

3rd Level

Ectoplasmic Attack - Throws a powerful ectoplasmic projectile.
Summon Psychic Entity - Brings psychic entities to the material world.

4th Level

Dimensional Anchor - Prevents movement between dimensions.
Dismiss - Forces one psychic entity back to its own dimension.

5th Level

Create Poltergeist - Creates one poltergeist in the real world.
Decay - Causes advanced rot or disease in the target.

6th Level

Banish - Forces psychic entities back to their own dimensions.

7th Level

Screams of the Damned - Unleashes horrific entities into the real world.

8th Level

Exorcise - Forces many psychic entities back to their own dimensions.
Psychoportation - Travel through dimensions to instantly teleport anywhere.

9th Level

Group Psychoportation - Teleports a number of allies anywhere in the world.

Pre-Cog Psi-Powers

0-Level

Precognitive Reflexes - Allows manifester to avoid small amounts of damage.

EVEN IF WE CAN PREDICT WHERE THEY'LL STRIKE NEXT, WHAT GOOD'LL IT DO? WE CAN DESTROY THEIR BODIES, BUT NOT THEIR SPIRIT FORMS.

THERE'S GOTTA SOME WEAPON WE CAN USE AGAINST THEM THERE'S GOTTA BE!

1st Level

Combat Precognition - Grants a +1 bonus to Defence Value.
Future Shock - Shocks the subject, doing 1d8 points of subdual damage.
Jinx - Curses an enemy.
Psychic Compass - Manifester always knows where he is.

2nd Level

Combat Prescience - Grants a +2 bonus to attack rolls.
Recall Injury - Forces a subject to take 3d6 points of subdual damage.

3rd Level

Sixth Sense - Temporarily grants the subject the Sixth Sense feat.

4th Level

Instant Precognition - Allows manifester to potentially avoid mishaps.

5th Level

True Sight - Subject sees things as they really are.

6th Level

Psi-Scan Trap - Sets a trap for those spying psychically.

7th Level

Sequester - Hides a subject from psychic sight.

8th Level

Foresight - Manifester cannot be surprised or ambushed.

9th Level

Epiphany - Gives answer to a question with total accuracy.

Pyrokine Psi-Powers

0 Level

Incinerating Finger - Creates a jet of flame that causes 1d3 points of damage.

1st Level

Searing Metal - Turns metal objects red hot.
Sheet of Flame - Sends a sheet of flame spreading outwards.

2nd Level

Control Flames - Forces fire to do manifester's bidding.
Flaming Weapon - Sets a melee weapon alight.

3rd Level

Pyrokinetic Burst - Creates a bright and powerful explosion.
Resist Flames - Manifester becomes immune to fire.

4th Level

Pyrokinesis - Causes a fire to throw our bright pyrotechnics.

5th Level

Fire of Retribution - Creates a column of fire.

6th Level

Flaming Shroud - Wraps a subject in burning flames.

7th Level

Incendiary Rounds - Creates a hail of incendiary fire.

8th Level

Rolling Fire - Creates a burning cloud that consumes everything in its path.
Tempest of Fire - Floods an area with a howling fire storm.

9th Level

Spontaneous Combustion - Causes any object to start burning from the inside ou.

Telekine Psi-Powers

0 Level

Minor Telekinesis - Weak version of *telekinesis*.

1st Level

Lightning Catch - Slows down a falling object.
Magnify Force - Puts telekinetic power behind manifester's blows.

2nd Level

Concussion - Blasts a target with 3d6 points of damage.
Control Body - Temporarily takes control of a victim's limbs.
Levitate - Causes a subject to rise or fall at manifester's whim.

3rd Level

Psychokinetic Shield - Grants 20 + 2d10 extra temporary hit points.

4th Level

Mass Concussion - More powerful version of *concussion*.
Telekinesis - Manifester can move objects with his mind alone.

5th Level

Concussive Blast - Blasts a target with 8d6 points of damage.

6th Level

Aggrokinesis - Rips a target apart, causing 10d6 points of damage.

7th Level

Greater Telekinesis - Improved version of *telekinesis*.

Summary

8th Level

Headjam - Causes a subject's head to explode.

9th Level

Crushing Force - Instantly crushes enemies to a pulp.

Telepath Psi-Powers

0 Level

Xenoglossia - Manifester communicates and understands any language.

1st Level

Attraction & Aversion - Plants compulsion in subject's mind.

Empathic Transfer - Transfers wounds and diseases from

subject to manifester.

Enrapture - Subject becomes trusted ally and friend to manifester.

2nd Level

Bind - Prevents subject from moving.

Mindlink - Forges telepathic link from manifester to subject.

Pain - Inflicts 3d6 points of telepathic pain upon a subject.

Suggestion - Compels subject to follow order.

3rd Level

Fabricated Reality - Changes a subject's perceptions.

4th Level

Domination - Utterly controls the actions of a subject.

Fatal Attraction - Implants death wish in subject.

Mindwipe - Destroys the subject's memories and experiences.

Tailor Memory - Creates a false memory in the subject's mind.

5th Level

Brain Drain - Drains a subject of 1d6 points of Charisma or Intelligence.

Psychic Static - Makes manifesting powers a lot more difficult.

Psychic Vampire - Drains power points from subject.

6th Level

Doppelganger - Manifester takes the appearance of someone else.

Mass Suggestion - Improved version of *suggestion*.

7th Level

Flense - Strips powers away from psi-talented characters.

Mass Domination - Improved version of *domination*.

8th Level

Secret World - Condemns a victim to explore a world of its own imagination.

9th Level

Confidante - Permanent version of *mindlink*.

Psychic Surgery - Repair any damage caused by psychic attacks.

Thrall - Utterly dominates the subject.

*   Psi-power detailed in the *Judge Dredd Rulebook*.

Psi-Feats

Feat	Prerequisite
Additional Power	-
Astral Projection	Manifest 5th level psi-powers
Body Fuel *	Inner Strength, Talented
Change Instruction	*Summon psychic entity*, specialist (dimensionalist)
Combat Manifestation *	Concentration skill
Defensive Block	Specialist Focus
Drain Psi-Talent	Mental Adversary
Greater Power Penetration *	Power Penetration
Greater Specialist Focus (any)	Specialist Focus, specialist
Improved Transformation	Transformation
Innate Power	Inner Strength, Talented
Inner Strength *	-
Longevity	Manifest 6th level psi-powers
Meditation	Manifest 3rd level psi-powers
Mental Adversary	Cha 13+
Mental Snare	*Mental shield, mind shield*
Permanent Control	Cha 15+, *summon psychic entity*, specialist (dimensionalist)
Power Penetration *	-
Precognitive Sense	Manifest 4th level psi-powers, specialist (pre-cog)
Psychic Inquisitor *	Cha 13+, Psychoanalyst
Psychoanalyst *	Cha 13+
Quicken Summoning	Int 15+, *summon psychic entity*, specialist (dimensionalist)
Specialist Focus	Specialist (any)
Strength of Will	Iron Will, *summon psychic entity*

Summary

Synergy	Manifest 4th level psi-powers
Talented *	Inner Strength
Telekinetic Punch	Specialist (telekinetic)
Transformation	Con 13+

Metapsi Feats

Feat	Prerequisite
Encompassing Power	-
Enhanced Power	-
Enlarge Power *	-
Extend Power *	-
Far Power	-
Hypnopathy	Wis 13+, *mindlink*, specialist (telepath)
Magnify Power	-
Maintain Power	Inner Strength, Talented
Maximise Power *	-
Necrospan *	-
Quicken Power *	-
Twin Power	-

* Feat detailed in the *Judge Dredd Rulebook*.

Possession Table

Will Save failed by	Time Possessed	Side Effects
1-3	1 hour	-1 Wis and Cha, -1,000 XP
4-8	1 day	-1d6 ability scores, -1,000 XP
9-12	1 year	-1d6 ability scores, - 1d6 x 1,000 XP
13+	Permanent	-2d6 ability scores, - 2d6 x 1,000 XP

Summoning Check Modifiers

Factor	Modifier
Expertise	+ psyker's character level
Study and Preparation	+ psyker's Intelligence modifier
Slow Summoning	+2
Hurried Summoning	-4

Control Check Modifiers

Factor	Modifier
Expertise	+ psyker's character level
Force of Will	+ psyker's Charisma modifier
Slow Summoning	+2
Hurried Summoning	-4
Blood Sacrifice	+1
Soul Sacrifice	+ sacrifice's character level
Additional Instructions	-2 cumulative
Multiple Summoning	-1 per entity
Possessing Others	-4